ART IN THE ROMAN EMPIRE

ART IN THE ROMAN EMPIRE

Michael Grant

London and New York

First published 1995
by Routledge
11 New Fetter Lane, London EC4P 4EE

Simultaneously published in the USA and Canada
by Routledge
29 West 35th Street, New York, NY 10001

© 1994 Michael Grant Publications Limited

Typeset in Garamond by
Datix International Limited, Bungay, Suffolk
Printed and bound in Great Britain by
Biddles Limited, Guildford and King's Lynn

British Library Cataloguing in Publication Data
A catalogue record for this book is available from the British Library

Library of Congress Cataloguing in Publication Data
A catalogue record for this book has been requested

ISBN 0-415-12031-4

$27.85 MW 8/19/96 (mc)

CONTENTS

LIST OF ILLUSTRATIONS

1. ITALY AND SICILY

0   km   200
0   miles   120

Comum

Aquileia

GALLIA CISALPINA   Verona

R. Padus

Luna

Ancona

ETRURIA

R. Tiber

ADRIATIC SEA

Fidenae
Rome
Ostia   Velitrae   Arpinum
Castel Porziano
LATIUM

Herculaneum   Mt.Vesuvius
Puteoli   Pompeii
        Stabiae

SARDINIA

SICILY
Piazza Armerina
Philosophiana

MEDITERRANEAN SEA

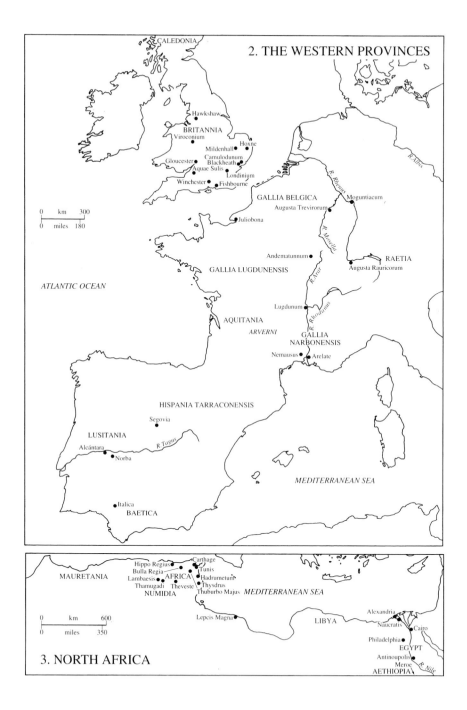

2. THE WESTERN PROVINCES

CALEDONIA

BRITANNIA
Hawkshaw
Viroconium
Mildenhall
Hoxne
Camulodunum
Gloucester
Blackheath
Aquae Sulis
Londinium
Winchester
Fishbourne
Juliobona

GALLIA BELGICA
Augusta Trevirorum
Moguntiacum

R. Rhenus

R. Albis

R. Mosella

RAETIA
Augusta Rauricorum

Andematunnum

GALLIA LUGDUNENSIS

ATLANTIC OCEAN

R. Arar

Lugdunum

R. Rhodanus

AQUITANIA

ARVERNI

GALLIA
NARBONENSIS
Nemausus
Arelate

HISPANIA TARRACONENSIS

Segovia

LUSITANIA
Alcántara
Norba

R. Tagus

MEDITERRANEAN SEA

Italica
BAETICA

km 300
miles 180

MAURETANIA

Hippo Regius
Carthage
Bulla Regia
Tunis
Lambaesis
AFRICA
Hadrumetum
Thamugadi
Theveste
Thysdrus
NUMIDIA
Thuburbo Majus
MEDITERRANEAN SEA

Lepcis Magna
LIBYA

Alexandria
Naucratis
Cairo

Philadelphia
EGYPT

Antinoupolis
Meroe
R. Nile
AETHIOPIA

km 600
miles 350

3. NORTH AFRICA

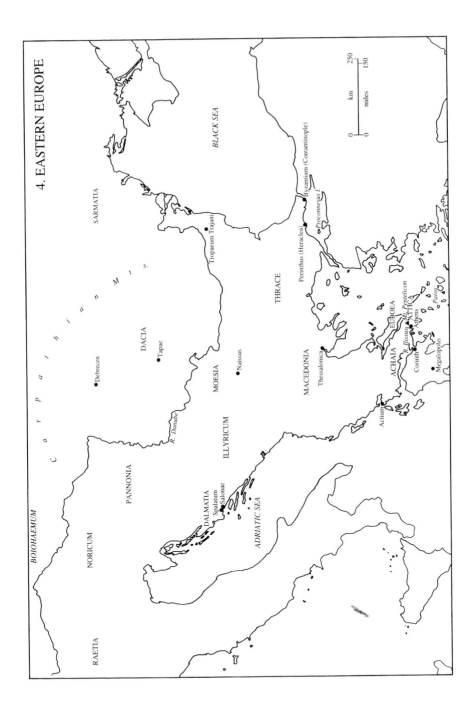

4. EASTERN EUROPE

BOIOHAEMUM

RAETIA

NORICUM

PANNONIA

SARMATIA

C a r p a t h i a n M t s.

DACIA

• Debrecen

• Tapae

R. Danube

ILLYRICUM

MOESIA

• Naissus

Tropaeum Trajani •

BLACK SEA

THRACE

Byzantium (Contantinople)

Perinthus (Heraclea) •

Proconnesus I.

DALMATIA

Spalatum
• Salonae

ADRIATIC SEA

MACEDONIA

Thessalonica •

Actium •

ACHAIA

EUBOEA

M. Pentelicon

R. Ilissus ATTICA

Corinth • Athens

Megalopolis

Paros

km

miles

250

150

0

0

xi

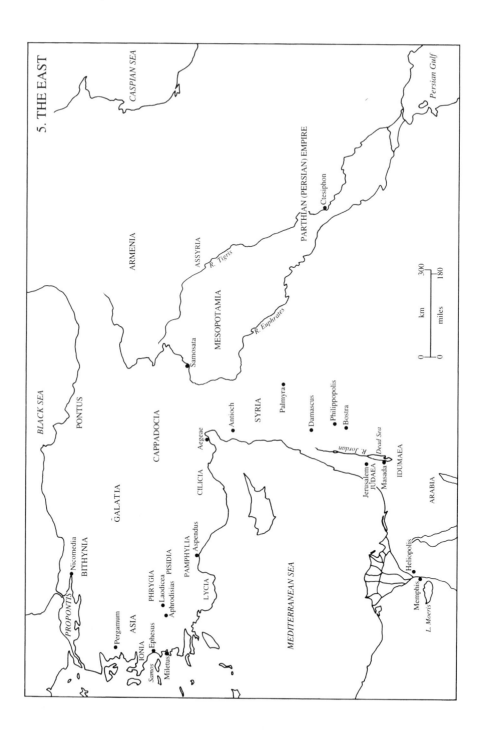

5. THE EAST

ACKNOWLEDGEMENTS

I am very grateful to the following who have helped me with this book: Emma
K. Baxter of the Cambridge University Press, Messrs Blackwell's, Dr Andrew
Burnett, Keeper of Coins and Medals at the British Museum, Sarah C. Butler,
Messrs David & Charles, Maria Ellis, W. E. Metcalf, Valeria Scott of the
British School at Rome, Professor Andrew Wallace-Hadrill (*Journal of Roman
Studies*), Richard Stoneman, Sarah-Jane Woolley and Victoria Peters of
Routledge, and my wife.

As regards the illustrations, I much appreciate the assistance and permissions
I have received from the Alaoui Museum, Tunis, the Bibliothèque Nationale,
Paris (M. Amandry), the British Museum (Photographic Service), Messrs Cassell,
the Detroit Institute of Arts (William H. Peck), the German Archaeological
Institute at Rome (Helmut Jung), the Museo Archeologico Nazionale (Naples),
the Palestine Exploration Fund (T. C. Mitchell), Penguin Books, the Rheinisches
Landesmuseum, Trier, the San Antonio Museum of Art (Gerry D. Scott III),
Richard Stoneman, the University of North Carolina Press (Kathy Shear),
Thames & Hudson International (Hans Coudenhove), the Vatican Museums
(Paolo Liverani), the Yale University Press (Robert Baldock).

I also owe an acknowledgement to the following for allowing me to include
quotations: Abbeville Press, for A. L. Croutier, *Taking the Waters* (New York:
1992); American Numismatic Society, for J. M. C. Toynbee, *Roman Medallions*
(amended reprint, ed. W. E. Metcalf, New York: 1986); B. T. Batsford Ltd, for
C. H. V. Sutherland, *Art in Coinage* (London: 1955) (Bobby Cox); George
Braziller Inc., for F. E. Brown, *Roman Architecture* (New York: 1961) (C. J.
Keyes); Cambridge University Press, for my *From Imperium to Auctoritas*
(Cambridge/London: 1946) and *Roman History from Coins* (Cambridge/London:
1958) (Linda Nicol); David Higham Associates, for R. Fedden, *Syria* (London:
Robert Hale, 1946); *Journal of Roman Studies*, for 'Palmyra under the aegis of the
Romans', by I. A. Richmond (1963); W. W. Norton, for G. M. A. Hanfmann,
Roman Art (New York: 1975); Orion Publishing Group, for my *World of Rome*
(London: 1960), *The Climax of Rome* (London: 1968), *Cities of Vesuvius* (London:
1971), *Herod the Great* (London: 1971), *The Visible Past* (London: 1990), *The
Emperor Constantine* (London: 1993); the Palestine Exploration Fund, for S.

Gibson and J. Taylor, *Beneath the Church of the Holy Sepulchre, Jerusalem* (London: 1994); Penguin Books, for R. Krautheimer, *Etruscan and Roman Architecture* (Pelican History of Art) (Harmondsworth, Mx: 1981 [1970]); Laurence Pollinger Ltd, for R. Fedden, *Syria* (London: Robert Hale, 1946); Society for the Promotion of Roman Studies, for 'Palmyra under the aegis of the Romans', by I. A. Richmond, in *Journal of Roman Studies* LIII (1963) (Dr Helen Cockle); Richard Stoneman, *Palmyra and its Empire* (Ann Arbor, MI: University of Michigan Press, 1992); Thames & Hudson International, for P. Fischer, *Mosaic: History and Technique* (London: 1971), A. Menen and R. Wood, *Cities in the Sand* (London: 1972) and S. Rozenberg, *Enchanted Landscapes: Wall Paintings from the Roman Era* (London: 1994); *Times Literary Supplement* (Alan Jenkins, Andrew Weir); University of Chicago Press (Jim Willis); University of North Carolina Press, for P. MacKendrick, *The Dacian Stones Speak* (Chapel Hill, NC: 1975) (K. Shaer); Professor Cornelius C. Vermeule III of the Museum of Fine Arts, Boston; Roger Wood.

INTRODUCTION

By the time that Augustus founded the Roman principate, after he had defeated Antony and Cleopatra at Actium in 31 BC and pursued them to their deaths in Egypt in the following year, the empire was already large, including Spain, Gaul, Africa (Tunisia), Greece, Asia (western Asia Minor), Pontus (northern Asia Minor) and Syria, to which Egypt was now added. So, later in the reign, were Galatia (25 BC) and Judaea (AD 6), and in the north Augustus advanced the frontier to the Danube and created a chain of provinces (Raetia, Noricum, Pannonia, Moesia) which protected the Balkans from invasion. But his plan to make the River Albis (Elbe) instead of the River Rhenus (Rhine) the imperial boundary was abandoned after the defeat of Varus (AD 9), and the Rhine-Danube formed the northern frontier, as the Euphrates constituted the frontier in the east. Across the rivers, however, as elsewhere on the imperial borders, there were client princedoms dependent on Rome.

Tiberius, the successor of Augustus, made Cappadocia a province (AD 17), in order to facilitate defence against Parthia, which at that time was the only major power bordering upon the Roman empire. Claudius (41–54) added the two Mauretanias, Britain, Lycia and Thrace. Under Nero, there were revolts in Britain (61) and Judaea (the First Jewish Revolt, 66–70). In the time of Domitian (81–96), the last of the three Flavians (Vespasian and Titus came before him), Decebalus of Dacia had to be recognized as an independent (even if 'client') ruler, but Trajan defeated him (101–2, 105–6) and annexed the country. He also annexed Nabataean Arabia in Transjordania, and advanced across the Euphrates to wrest from Parthian control the new provinces of Armenia, Mesopotamia and Assyria, although these were soon lost (Mesopotamia was later regained). Hadrian (117–38) constructed his Wall in northern Britain (122–7), established Upper and Lower Germany as separate provinces, and put down the Second Jewish Revolt (132–5). Antoninus Pius built a second British Wall farther north (142–3, soon abandoned), and Marcus Aurelius (161–80) planned to extend the continental frontier north of the Danube to the Carpathians and mountains of Boiohaemum (Bohemia), but his son Commodus (180–2) abandoned the project.

The third century AD was a grim period for the empire, which was menaced by amalgamated German tribes from the north and by the Sassanian Persians who succeeded the Parthians in the east, overran Syria, captured the Emperor Valerian (259), and invaded Asia Minor. Miraculously, a series of soldier emperors stemmed the tide (although one of the greatest of them, Aurelian (270–5), evacuated Dacia), and the empire was reconstituted by Diocletian (284–305), who created a tetrarchic system of government consisting of two Augusti and two Caesars. Diocletian, before abdicating in 305, had set up his court at Nicomedia (Izmit). Then Constantine I the Great (306–37) refounded Byzantium as Constantinople and established Christianity as the state religion. Valentinian I (364–75) divided the empire into two parts, western and eastern, of which the former ceased to exist in 476 – taken over by the Germans; the latter, based on Constantinople, continued to survive and flourish as the Byzantine empire (after an interruption in the thirteenth century) until 1453.

There have been a good many books about the art of the Romans, but I think there is room for one more, with the title and subject that I have allotted to this present volume. I have chosen the title *Art in the Roman Empire*, rather than the more usual one of *Roman Art*, because I want readers to appreciate that all the art of the Roman empire was not concentrated in Rome. Rome is a miraculous city, full to bursting with ancient Roman objects and buildings, but an enormously large portion of the art of the ancient Romans is to be found not only in Rome itself but in its provinces, and due attention should be given – and is not always given – to what is to be found in those provinces, in addition to what exists in Rome. The influence of the art of Rome upon the art of its provinces is an interesting and highly complex question. And so is the opposite phenomenon, which sometimes makes its appearance – the influence of provincial art upon the art of Rome.

But there are also elements in provincial art, sometimes, which do not come from Rome, or go to Rome, at all. These elements are of various, local origins.[1] Of course the best known and most obvious and famous of such phenomena is the influence of Greece upon Rome. Here misunderstandings often occur, sometimes inspired by the designation of 'classical art', which is intended to cover the art both of Greece and of Rome. The designation has an unmistakable meaning and value, because the two arts, mirroring the classical world that produced them, do hang together to a considerable extent, particularly in contrast to what preceded and followed them. And it is perfectly arguable, indeed practically certain, that there would have been no Roman art at all if it had not been able to develop under Greek influences.[2]

The comparative uniformity which thus developed, observed Ludwig Friedländer,

> can only be partly explained by the migration of artists and the production of works of art for commercial purposes. Its chief cause was the finished development of Greek art at the time when it first entered into the service of Roman civilization. This development had been unprecedented. It had

produced an immense wealth of form and ideas, and had brought to perfection a many-sided method of treatment and representation.[3]

The relationship of the Romans to the Greeks was a curious love–hate affair. Of course, we cannot tell what the ordinary, non-literary, non-literate Roman felt about the Greeks, but we can guess that he or she did not estimate them very highly; after all, Rome had conquered them. As to more cultured contemporaries, their feeling towards the Greeks was ambivalent. On the one hand, Romans never lost sight of the fact that Rome had been Greece's conqueror; they thought (rightly) that Greek law was nothing like as good as Roman, and they regarded the city-states as small-scale and parochial. But on the other hand an unbounded admiration was felt for the Greek past, with all its literary and artistic traditions. What Romans thought of the numerous, travelling Greek artists and architects of their own time, who had built up their own world, we scarcely know. But we can guess, perhaps, that while they would not have wanted to invite such persons to dinner they admired their artistic and cultural capabilities.

However, Friedländer, as we shall see, overestimated the degree to which the art of the Roman empire was uniform. Nevertheless, his emphasis on its Greek antecedents is fully justified. It has sometimes been deduced from this undoubted fact that Roman art is merely a subdivision, or an appendix, of Greek art, an inferior sequel, a lesser offspring.[4] Yet that is manifestly not the case. The art of the Roman empire, even if some of it was of poor quality (the same applies to all arts of all peoples), and much of it was predominantly ostentatious, contains sensational features and qualities which are entirely alien to what the Romans had learned from the Greeks, and which are, in other words, original.

This point deserves to be dwelt on a little. We talk of the 'Greco-Roman civilization', and Greece and Rome do, in a sense, form a unity, the unity that is the ancient, classical world. Moreover, as has been suggested, the debt of Rome to Greece was unimaginably enormous. Rome, and Roman architecture and art, could never have existed at all if it had not been for the Greeks before them. And yet the Romans made something new out of what they inherited from the Greeks, in very many fields. I think that if you had asked the average, fairly cultured Roman what he thought about the Greeks he would have spoken very much as Cicero wrote: that Greek tradition was wonderful and unique, but that living Greeks (like their law) were not up to much. This was understandable, since the Romans so emphatically held the upper hand, but in the artistic and architectural fields it was perhaps a little unfair. For one thing, it may be suspected that so many of Rome's artists and architects, even if we cannot nowadays identify them, were Greeks or had a Greek training. Nevertheless, the Romans had a point. They owed a gigantic amount to the Greeks, but they had made something new and original out of their Greek heritage, with the help, very often, not only of earlier Etruscan influences, but of other, widespread, local traditions as well.

This Roman originality is notable in a variety of different fields, among which is architecture: and I have had no hesitation in including architecture among the arts of the Roman empire.[5] The architects of our own time insist variously that architecture is an art and a science. I doubt if Roman architects did the same, but their wonderful products, despite all their practical uses and monumental impressiveness, possess pronounced artistic features, and wholly deserve to be considered in any treatment of the arts.

But our idea of what an artist is does not correspond at all exactly with what the ancient Romans meant by *artifex*. The centuries in between have distanced us irreparably from the Roman epoch, in which there had been only the slightest difference between artist and artisan. The Romans saw as an *artifex* not only the man (there were also some women involved)[6] who made an original work of art but also anybody who was engaged in the pursuit of an *ars*; that is to say, anybody who undertook work which demanded a specific fund of technical information. Many may consider it surprising that peoples like the Romans, who were manifestly so imperialistic, together with the numerous races and nations in the provinces which they brought into being in order to make their empire, should have produced such superb art. And it is, perhaps, surprising. But that is what the Romans were like. They were imperialists, and yet they produced and inspired great artists – artists as great, even if often nowadays unidentifiable, as any whom the world has seen since.

One reason, therefore, for studying the art and architecture of the Roman empire is that they are so good; they are in many ways better than anything that preceded or followed them. But another reason for studying them is that they have such a close link with the latter phenomenon – with what followed them. Or, to be more specific, what followed them to a large extent echoed and copied what the Romans had done. And that still applies to ourselves today. The art and architecture of the present day, our own work, would be far poorer had not its creators taken so much from the Romans. In other words, Roman art is not only good and interesting in itself, but is also the source of a great deal of our modern artistic production. And this applies not only to Rome but to the Roman world as a whole. That world is, in itself, an astonishing unit or group of units, but it is also infinitely worth studying because it is so very much our own precursor. This is clearly true, moreover, not only of the Roman world as a whole but also of the art which fulfilled such an important role in that world. Yet we can forget this debt, if we like. Because the art of the Roman empire is so good in itself – without considering what we ourselves owe to it.

Ah, but it is the product of imperialism, and imperialism is so distinctly out of fashion today. True, the art of the Roman world was either influenced by Rome, or influenced it, through artistic movements and developments trickling in to the capital from the conquered provinces. But, in any case, is the sort of imperialism practised by the Romans really so totally out of fashion and irrelevant today? Certainly, the top nations (or top nation, if we reckon there is only one, namely the United States of America) do not, or does not, any longer convert conquered territories into provinces. But there seems to be a definite parallel, well worth considering, between the ancient Roman state, extending from the Atlantic Ocean to the Euphrates, and the modern Europe, which is taking shape in an area stretching from the Atlantic in the west to points still disputed and undetermined far to the east. Of course, the frontiers of the two vast units are different. Even leaving aside the uncertainty about the eastern borders of the modern entity, it is at least likely to cover a far more easterly and north-easterly region than its ancient counterpart, which notoriously became stuck on the Rhenus (Rhine) and, for much of the time, on the Danube, failing to reach eastwards (except for a very few years) even as far as the Albis (Elbe) – just as, outside Europe, it failed to assert itself on the Persian Gulf. Nevertheless, although 'imperialism' is nowadays so out of date, the ancient and modern models do have a good deal in common. In particular, each covers a vast area, including a whole multitude of different countries, races, customs and languages.

And that is partly why the art of the Roman empire deserves such careful study. For there were distinct similarities, as well as local dissimilarities, in the arts of all these regions, and the role that the Roman epicentre and government played in this variegated picture is one of the matters that most needs examining (although one can be quite sure of one thing, which is that it was very different from the role which Brussels or Strasbourg will play today – partly because we have had centuries of nation-states since Roman times).

Whatever comparisons one may wish to make with modern times, in the Roman age,

> For the first – and last – time in history, the Mediterranean was politically as well as culturally one world. Along with unification under a single ruler, there came, after centuries of almost continuous bloodshed, the rare and precious gift of peace, close to two hundred years of it. . . . And so, the first two centuries of the Christian era were halcyon days for a traveller.[7]

But there is one serious obstacle, though it does provide an additional reason why, in my view, this book needs to be written. That obstacle lies in the fact that there was a very great deal of art created in the huge Roman empire – and an extremely large amount of it is still to be seen.

> The Romans, who in general had no idea of the real and independent value of art, regarded it only as one means among others of refining the enjoyments of life and of perpetuating the memory of persons and things. If we only possessed the two literatures, we should have no idea of what the fine arts even then were capable of producing, nor of the astonishing extent to which the need of artistic ornamentation and monumental representation had pervaded all classes of society, nor the enormous

development of activity which it called forth in sculpture and painting. Yet how rich was this civilization, which was accustomed to dispose of the productions of art to an extent inconceivable to the modern world, which reckoned among the least of its possessions and carelessly scattered broadcast those treasures, whose immensity humiliates us and fills us with astonishment![8]

In other words, it must be repeated, the artistic creations and remains of the Roman empire are appallingly, abominably extensive. That is why books on the subject sometimes seem jumbled and make depressing reading: for they try to be too comprehensive. What one has to aim at instead, and what the reader surely requires, is selectivity. And so I have avoided attempting yet another general handbook, and have instead tried my best to be selective. Out of all the thousands of works of art and architecture I have selected only between thirty and forty. Others might have selected different works, but this is my personal choice among them all. I have singled out works that seem to me pre-eminently important.

And I have divided the works that I have selected into three categories. Part I, which deals with the first of these categories, is concerned with the art of portrait sculpture, giving attention, although this is so Roman an art, to its manifestations outside Italy. Chapter 1, concentrating on imperial portraiture, discusses the head of Augustus from far-distant Meroe, now in the British Museum, as well as one or two of the imperial portraits that were made in the provinces and a bust of that very un-Roman emperor Philip 'the Arabian' in the Vatican; and something is said of the active provincial school of sculpture at Aphrodisias. Chapter 2, devoted to non-imperial portraiture, deals largely with the sculptural heads and figures of Palmyra: thus illustrating the manner in which some of the most distinguished sculptors of the day depicted non-Romans. Chapter 3 turns to reliefs, and gives prominence to those on the Trophy of Trajan at Adamklissi in Rumania (Tropaeum Trajani). But before long by far the most important relief work appeared on sarcophagi, and that is the theme of Chapter 4, in which special attention is paid to a sarcophagus found at Velletri (Velitrae), not so very long ago.

Part II of the book has architecture as its theme – architecture, as I have said, regarded, as the Romans very actively and successfully regarded it, as one of the arts. Chapter 5 is concerned with pagan temples, and particularly with the great shrine of Jupiter-Baal and other divinities at Heliopolis (Baalbek) in Phoenicia. Chapter 6 turns to houses, describing those at Pompeii, Herculaneum and Ostia, and the grander mansions of Herod the Great at Masada and of a late Roman at Piazza Armerina (Philosophiana) in Sicily and at Spalatum (Split, near Salonae) in Dalmatia (Diocletian's palace). Chapter 7 brings together a number of different sorts of places of entertainment, including libraries (the library of Celsus at Ephesus [Selçuk], baths (Aquae Sulis in Britain), theatres (at Aspendus in Pamphylia), amphitheatres (at Nemausus [Nîmes]), and stadia (the stadium of

Herodes Atticus at Athens). Chapter 8 passes on to arches (the 'Arch of Trajan' at Thamugadi [Timgad]), bridges (Alcántara between Hispania Tarraconensis and Lusitania) and aqueducts (Segovia). The subject of Chapter 9 is that very Roman institution the pagan basilica, exported, in varying forms, to Lepcis Magna (Lebda) in Libya, Augusta Trevirorum (Trier) on the River Mosella (Moselle),and the Basilica of Maxentius (Constantine) at Rome itself. Chapter 10 points to some of the achievements of Christian architecture, notably the longitudinal 'basilica' (St John Studios at Constantinople, and the much altered St Peter's and S. Maria Maggiore at Rome), and the centralized *martyrium* (of which traces survive in the church of the Anastasis [Resurrection], or Holy Sepulchre, at Jerusalem).

Part III groups together the other arts. Thus Chapter 11 discusses paintings, with special reference to the Lost Ram from Pompeii at Naples Museum. Chapter 12 notes the significance of mosaics, dwelling upon the mosaic of Dominus Julius from Carthage in the Bardo (Alaoui) Museum at Tunis. Chapter 13 says something about coins, singling out Hadrian's issues commemorating the provinces, and writes of medallions, among which those of Antoninus Pius preparing for the ninth centenary of Rome seem particularly noteworthy. Chapter 14 takes gems and jewellery as its subject, describing the Gemma Augustea and the ear-rings found at Mampsis. Chapter 15 deals with silverware, particularly emphasizing the Great Dish that formed part of the Mildenhall Treasure from Suffolk. An epilogue seeks to sum the whole matter up.

*   *   *

As some of the remarks in the foregoing pages have suggested, the question of the Romanness, or otherwise, of the art of the Roman empire is a very complicated one. Sometimes the taste and practice of Rome prevailed; sometimes local features took over and predominated. And even at Rome itself things were not all that simple, because many Greeks and Asians had flocked into the imperial city and stamped its art with their own regional or personal characteristics. Since most of these men, and so much of the art of the Roman empire, was and remained anonymous, it is extremely hard to reconstruct what actually happened. There has been a lot of discussion about this question of the 'nationality' of the artists in the Roman world – sculptors, architects, mosaicists, gem-engravers, metal-workers. Most of those about whom we have literary evidence had Greek names, so that they were either Greek by origin or at least easterners who had some knowledge of Greek. There must, of course, have been others. Yet the guidelines of Roman imperial art, as was suggested earlier, were fundamentally Greek.

However, both in the west and the east, along the fringes of the Roman world, indigenous cultures continued to assert themselves against Greco-Roman traditions. These local persistences remained emphatic, and affected the reception and absorption of Greco-Roman influences. Moreover, local artistic centres became distinguished and powerful – notably at Lugdunum (Lyon) in the west, and at Aphrodisias in Asia.

For Rome itself was far away. Yet it did produce official models and send them out to the provincial communities. And this meant that, in spite of and sometimes at war with local ways of doing things, something like a common sort of art, an aesthetic commonwealth or *koine*, came into existence, just as, in the political field, the *Pax Romana* itself tended towards the foundation of a Roman *koine*, from at least the first century BC or the first century AD. Yet this *koine* remained something distinctly loose and flexible, in which variety and diversity found no difficulty in continuing to survive. In other words, Roman-ness made its appearance and became accepted, but regional and local traditions continued to exist for all that, and need to be noted.

Nevertheless, against the enormous diversity of the various regions, there was also a strong drive towards unity, to which Pliny the Elder eloquently testified: 'the might of the Roman empire has made the world the possession of all: human life has profited by the exchange of goods and the blessings of peace.'[9]

In this process, however, the society of the empire radically altered and widened. Freed slaves and immigrants from conquered lands took part in its transformation, and changed its culture considerably.

Part I

SCULPTURE

I

IMPERIAL PORTRAITS

As early as the third millennium BC, Egypt and the cities on the Persian Gulf had developed effective methods of portrait sculpture. Much later on, during the last centuries BC, a number of different phenomena in the Greco-Roman world contributed to the revival and further evolution of this art. The Greeks of the epochs of Alexander III the Great (d. 323 BC) and his successors, the Hellenistic monarchs, had a liking for human documents of a biographical or autobiographical character. This tendency was stimulated by a fashion for philosophical reflection and self-analysis, as well as by the enhancement of hero-worship, and the growing interest in personalities which such trends encouraged.

In other words, the Hellenistic epoch was an age of enhanced concern for the individual. In contrast to the Greek sculptors of classical times, who had endeavoured to present a human being as a focus of generalization, the artists who came after them sought to emphasize and stress the unique characteristics of whatever man or woman they were depicting. Like the biographers who were their contemporaries, these Hellenistic artists meticulously took note of contrasting and ambiguous characteristics in the personages whom they depicted, and of the coexistence in them of factors that seemed to be contradictory.

Their concentration on such aspects was stimulated by a study which was very much *à la mode* in these Hellenistic years – physiognomy. Originating as a branch of Greek medicine, ascribed to the fifth-century physician Hippocrates, this science, or pseudo-science, had come into favour during the century which followed. One of its subdivisions was zoological, pointing out the analogies between human beings and animals, and another was ethnic, seeking to define the distinctive peculiarities of races or peoples by consideration of their physical differences. Students of physiognomy also took note of revelations of personal character through facial expressions (a critic of this technique pointed out that if you applied it to Socrates he turned out to be stupid and keen on women!). The best-known authority on physiognomy was Antonius Polemo (*c.* AD 88–144), a popular philosopher or sophist from Laodicea (Pamukkale) in Phrygia (Asia Minor), whose writings were destined, subsequently, to exercise an influence on Islamic writers.

These were the elements which – augmented by the survival of a number of much earlier Egyptian busts – created a new efflorescence of portrait sculpture in the Hellenistic world. True, by way of contrast to the abundance of heads and portrait-statues of later Roman epochs that have come down to us, relatively few from the last centuries BC are now extant. Yet certain Hellenistic artists, such as the creator of the portrait of the Indo-Greek monarch Euthydemus I Theos (c. 220 BC), or the originator of studies of an old and brutalized fisherman of which later versions are extant, or the portrayer of King Mithridates VI of Pontus (d. 63 BC) (in a more idealized form) upon coins, can still be seen – and are so excellent that it was hard for their successors to do any better.[1]

That was not, however, for want of trying, and the last century BC was a period when the renewed and increased impact of Greek sculpture upon the family traditions of eminent Romans brought remarkable developments in portraiture into existence. They took place because of the massive financial incentives which those Romans offered: they were among the most notable and lucrative patrons of the arts that the world has ever produced. Those portions of Latin literature which still survive frequently allude to the decoration of the mansions and villas of distinguished Romans with Greek works of art – including portrait-busts.

And these houses contained numerous copies as well: for Romans who could afford to do so commissioned copies of these Greek artistic productions of all periods, from the sixth century BC onwards – thus preserving for posterity, at least in their main features, numerous masterpieces made by the Greeks. It must be admitted that these copies in Roman mansions did not invariably achieve perfection. For their creators were not always fully aware of the methods that a Greek artist had employed, or of the full nature of his achievement. Such ancient art-criticism as has come down to us too often fails to display a great deal of insight. Let us consider, for example, Pliny the Elder, who is probably one of the best of the critics, although both his knowledge and his taste are faulty. The greatest sculptor, according to him, had been Lysippus of Sicyon, the selected portrayer of Alexander III the Great. But Pliny was of the opinion that all paintings and bronzework were excelled by the later Laocoon Group, that unrestrained, tormentedly baroque creation that was one of the last important Hellenistic originals, the work of Rhodian sculptors of the second century BC (although it is possible that the version which we possess is a copy from the first century AD).[2]

Most leading Romans possessed much less knowledge of art than Pliny, yet they 'knew what they liked', and, by offering good money, set a vast and demanding task to the Greek and other sculptors of the last century BC onwards. What these potential employers wanted most of all was portraits; and something will be said about the artistic successes that resulted – that is to say, something will be said about the portraits of private citizens – in the next chapter.

The importance of art in the Roman empire, from the time when the principate began in the latter half of the first century BC, can best be understood through the medium of portraiture. And this was appreciated in no uncertain fashion by one Roman emperor after another, starting with the first of them, Augustus, who as a vital element in his introduction of the vast imperial system, based on his own personality cult, arranged that portrait-busts of himself should appear throughout all parts of his empire, as well as in the 'client' states that extended beyond its frontiers.[3] The artists who so cleverly designed these portraits are almost always unknown, but probably, as hitherto, they were mainly Greeks or at least trained by people versed in the Greek tradition. Acting, no doubt, on orders, or at least conscious of what was required of them, they presented Augustus in a range of different ways: as a modest and constitutionally minded Italian, as priest of one of the antique Roman cults, as a great military commander, or as a grand ruling figure in the line of Alexander III the Great.

One such bronze portrait[4] (Figure 1), somewhat in the last-named tradition (though no doubt owing much to an original Roman commission), was found as far away as the royal palace at Meroe, capital of the Aethiopian (Ethiopian) kingdom, which Roman forces had reduced to a precarious state of dependency. This head, full of tension and passion, portrays Augustus at the age of about 30, and may be contemporary (unless it dates from when he was older, towards the end of his reign), being taken from one of the many statues of him in military uniform, which were to be seen throughout the Roman world. The eyes have glass pupils in a bronze setting, with irises in black and yellow stone: they recall the assertion of Suetonius that Augustus took a great pride in the piercing majesty of his gaze.[5] Here, the evocation of the emperor is in the monarchical, Alexander tradition. Indeed, he is seen as a sort of radiant divinity, raised above the real facts of life and of the empire he had knitted together or reinstituted, in a manner which seems to divorce his material being from the reality of the world.

And this great tradition of Roman imperial portraiture continued unabated from the time of Augustus onwards.

> A likeness of the ruling prince, as an object of general cult, was to be seen in every camp and city. . . . After the middle of the third century (perhaps even at the beginning of the empire), it was the custom to send laurel-wreathed and (probably) painted likenesses of a new emperor into the provincial cities. Their arrival was announced by sound of trumpets, a long line of soldiers preceded the richly dressed bearer of the effigy, and the people went out to meet him with lights and censers. . . . Statues and images of the ruling prince were found throughout the empire, and were especially numerous in all the more important places. . . . Private individuals also were obliged to show their loyalty in this way. . . .

Figure 1 Bronze head of Augustus (31 BC–AD 14) from Meroe in northern Aethiopia (Ethiopia). British Museum.

Augustus had his portrait-busts sent to every village in the empire, and beyond its frontiers as well; and they were also copied locally. Like the coins (which circulated even more freely because they were smaller and cheaper), the busts were seen everywhere, and made it certain that the emperor's features were familiar to everyone. Sculptors were also careful to represent him in a variety of different lights. This bronze head, with fierce eyes, possibly part of a full-length statue, found at Meroe, across the Egyptian frontier, was perhaps a gift from the emperor to Rome's client monarch in the northern part of formerly hostile Aethiopia; just as there were client-rulers across many sections of the vast imperial frontiers. Here the emperor is seen as a grand, Alexander-like, imperial conqueror and ruler.

During the age of the Antonines [second century AD], the imperial images were to be seen everywhere, 'in the money-changers' offices, in the shops and workshops, under the eaves, in the vestibules, and at the windows'. Certainly, as a rule they were . . . coarsely modelled; but those in wealthy and distinguished houses were no doubt of superior workmanship. For then, in the larger cities, it was by no means uncommon for private individuals to set up statues of the emperors in public. . . . The rapid and enormous circulation of the imperial images cannot be adequately explained by their conveyance from a number of different centres. . . . A host of artists and artisans . . . poured into Rome from the provinces and back again.[6]

The portraits were often tinted, although the colours have now disappeared.

At all times, then, the government made a special effort to keep their massive subject-populations thoroughly well informed about the ceremonial activities of the emperor's life; and particular efforts were made to show everyone his features. . . . No modern dictator distributes his portraits so thoroughly as the Roman 'Fathers of their Country' circulated theirs. It was more important for them than for any modern regime to multiply the portraits of the ruler, for these were respected and venerated by the Romans, for religious reasons, to an altogether special and extraordinary extent – perhaps paralleled only in Japan.

So a Roman emperor ensured that there should be a variety of sculptured figures and heads of himself in great numbers in every town and village of the empire. We know of stringent rules against removing or damaging them. For the image of the emperor was sacred: to deface it or treat it lightly was treason: that is why such an effort was made, in every branch of visual art, to create a series of official portraits that were striking, characteristic and recognisable. Sometimes, though not always, realism was the aim. Sometimes the likenesses were excessively flattering. But on other occasions they were not: and it seems strange that the portraits of Nero and Caracalla, for example, should apparently have contented those emperors.[7]

A good example of a find in a remoter part of the Roman empire is provided by a bronze head of Hadrian (AD 117–38) recovered from the Thames at London Bridge and now in the British Museum. The question of its origin has been discussed.

The head [writes J. M. C. Toynbee] is certainly not Romano-British work . . . nor can we definitely class it as metropolitan. . . . The exceptionally broad and heavy face, the extreme stylization of the rows of curls above the brow, and the curious treatment of the back hair, have a provincial look; and the possibility remains that the artist was Gaulish and that the portrait was imported from one of the Gaulish provinces, if it were not cast in Britain by a craftsman invited over for the purpose by the authorities of Roman London.[8]

This problem of who made that portrait and where, raises general questions. The Meroe head of Augustus had been rather exceptional, because it was found right outside the empire. It must be remembered, however, that imperial portraits also appeared in every Roman province as well. In order that this purpose should be fulfilled, three different methods were employed. Images of the emperor and his relatives, or models, were sent out from Rome. Native artists in the provinces imitated these models – occasionally, no doubt, they were immigrants and travellers,[9] but mostly they were local people. And, thirdly, other artists in the same category, not having received such models or, having received them remaining dissatisfied with them as suitable responses to the needs of the province to which they belonged, undertook to make portraits of the emperor and his relatives themselves, not always wholly in keeping with what Rome had prescribed or would prescribe. So the process of ensuring that imperial images were to be found everywhere was a somewhat complicated one. It has been analysed in detail by Paul Zanker,[10] who has concentrated heavily on the reign of Hadrian and on his immediate successors the Antonines, although his conclusions, in general, would be equally valid for other periods as well, even if information about them would be harder (or impossible) to obtain. But his work is of value, particularly because it endeavours to draw a line between the three categories of portrait mentioned above, and because, also, it indicates how, and to what extent, the requirements and responses of one region differ from those of another.

The climax was reached in the third century, when the turn of the head of Caracalla (211–17) was something new, and although this was a time of political and military crisis and decline, portrait-busts of Maximinus I (235–8) and Philip (244–9) achieved extraordinary merit. Neither of them was a Roman: Maximinus originated from Thrace, and Philip came from a village named Philippopolis after him (Shahba), twelve miles from Bostra (Bosra Eski Sham); so that he was 'the Arabian'. The artists, then, whoever they were – and we do not know – at this juncture had the opportunity of savouring the multiple, multiracial character of the Roman world by the depiction of imperial leaders who were far from belonging to the empire's Italian, Roman core,[11] at a time when the whole imperial complex was in a state of the most acute political and military crisis, markedly contrasting with the confident and masterly skill displayed by the sculptors.

The bust of Philip in the Vatican Museum is particularly revealing (Figure 2).[12] It faces up to harsh reality without any concession, but was evidently made by a curiously sensitive artist. The eyes look upwards, as though seeking heavenly inspiration,[13] not downwards and sideways, as Caracalla, earlier, had been made to gaze or glance.

Figure 2 Marble bust of Philip the Arabian (AD 244–9) found at Porcigliano (Castel Porziano, Casale Tor Paterno) in Latium (Lazio). Vatican Museums (Braccio Nuovo).

One of the major glories of the Roman artistic achievement was its portraiture of emperors. The whole concept underwent a number of changes, which were also reflected by portraits made outside Rome and Italy; and these often exhibited local and personal variations of their own. One of the most significant developments occurred during the third century AD. Politically things were terrible, but the portrait artists – whoever they were: probably not Romans, but we do not know – made the most of the harrowed features of successive rulers. Philip was an interesting subject not only because of his nervous, anxious expression but because he was neither Roman nor Italian, but a near-eastern chieftain from what was then north-eastern Arabia (Nabataea).

[Philip's] strength of character is expressed through the long, bony, Semitic nose, his thick-lipped mouth and his deeply lined face. Perhaps most remarkable of all is the way in which the artist was able to capture here a moment of time, as if the emperor's face were moving, and the particular, fleeting expression had been caught in stone. Such skill is one of the great achievements of third-century portraiture.[14]

With a great simplifying touch, this artist has managed to concentrate physiognomical life in one characteristic sweep. The central motif is the threatening lowering of the brows, corresponding to convulsions of the forehead muscles and responding to nervous contractions of the muscles of the mouth. The psychological picture achieves an almost disturbing intensity. Behind the quivering features the very expression seems to change and move, flashing like a flickering flame over the face.

The artist has simplified and generalized the lines of Philip's countenance. There is a new, rather uncanny tension between naturalism and schematization, which is characteristic of the age, and which helps to explain why its portraiture is so good. It was an age of grim, stern happenings, and the details of such portraits seem deliberately intended to convey the strain, stress and fear of the epoch. And at the same time they vividly bring before us the provincial or foreign origins of many of the military men who became emperors during this time.

The bust of Philip was found at Porcigliano (Castel Porziano, Casale Tor Paterno) in Latium (Lazio), where it presumably adorned a house of the emperor, or of someone who supported him, or wanted it to be seen that he did. Perhaps the bust was made locally. Or perhaps it was not (and the same applies to many busts that are now at Rome).[15] But this portrait-bust of Philip does possess a metropolitan-seeming excellence of execution. Unfortunately, as usual, we have no idea who made it. As a pure guess, one would hazard that it was a non-Roman – a Greek or an easterner who had come to the west. Earlier busts of Roman emperors had been made by provincials, putting forward their own interpretations and points of view within the general framework of an imperial direction. But here we have someone portraying, with stunning skill and freedom, an emperor who was not a Roman or an Italian at all. This is not the first time that such a thing had happened: there is, as we saw, a very illuminating bust of a slightly earlier emperor who was a Thracian, Maximinus I. But the process reaches its full maturity under this Arab, Philip.

Towards the end of the third century which had produced these superb heads, portraiture stiffened into the hieratic art that is exemplified by the huge, scarcely personal head of Constantine I the Great (AD 306–37).[16] There had already been smouldering, frowning, nightmarish statues of the tetrarchs promoted to imperial status by Diocletian, such as the fear-inspiring pairs in Venice and the Vatican, and a red porphyry bust of Maximinus II Daia (d. AD 313) or Licinius (d. AD 324) at Cairo. But Constantine's enormous marble head, seven times life-size, now to be seen in the courtyard of the Conservatori Museum at Rome, is more imposing still. It formed part of a statue whose fabulous dimensions were in themselves intended to impress and overawe, workmanship apart. And, furthermore, this bust of Constantine has mobilized the remains of classicism to infuse a sinister touch of realism into its ritualistic, generalized pattern, which is reinforced by surrealistically, transcendentally huge, upward-gazing eyes, and by formidably aloof, exaggerated, scarcely mortal-looking features. An effort is being made to show a man in close contact with God.[17]

THE APHRODISIAN SCHOOL

One local school, a particularly flourishing one, had been active in the early days of the empire at Aphrodisias in Caria.[18] Inscribed bases in its North Portico bear the names of Augustus's grandsons and prospective heirs Gaius and Lucius, and of Drusus the Younger, son of Tiberius. These statues are lost, but others from the same school have survived (Figure 3), and there is evidence that Aphrodisias was not only an important marble supplier but also, throughout the imperial epoch, the productive home of a native school of sculptors, partly traditional and partly original. 'Their specific links were with the sculpture of Pergamum, so the school can be regarded as the logical, and even the organic, continuation of Pergamene art.'[19] And these Aphrodisian sculptors differed from their counterparts in Rome by vigorously incising the outlines of what they made, decorating their backgrounds and sharpening contrasts of lighting, since these statues were intended to exist under the powerful and ever-changing light of the sun. Moreover, behind such stylistic considerations there was also a practical point, based on the materials that were locally available. For whereas the white Greek marbles utilized at Rome for official sculptures were compact and possessed a delicate graining, the marbles of Aphrodisias were coloured and their grain was coarse, requiring in consequence a less refined and more baroque kind of treatment.

It has also been argued that this workshop was mobile and ambulatory, so the Aphrodisian sculptors went elsewhere (notably, as we shall see, to Lepcis Magna in North Africa). And their sculptural style is close to that of other centres in western Asia Minor, not far from Aphrodisias itself.[20]

*   *   *

Imperial portraits, then, display the interaction of the various regions of the Roman empire in a curious form. Their inspiration was, ultimately, Roman and imperial, Rome being the city where the emperors resided and ruled. But the rest of the empire, too, enters into the matter, in a variety of different ways. First of all, as we saw, these busts were displayed in the remotest village of the remotest province, and even carried beyond the imperial frontiers themselves. Secondly, they were reduplicated and adapted in those far-off areas – showing

Figure 3 Marble portrait bust from Aphrodisias, *c.* AD 100. Probably an imperial personage? Or not?

the emperor in whatever guise he desired to adopt, after due adjustment to the characters and tastes of the people of the region in question. Thirdly, the emperors themselves were, as time went on, less and less likely to be Romans: we have seen that Philip was an 'Arab'. And fourthly, the sculptors who so cleverly designed these portraits, even if they worked at Rome, were unlikely to be Roman. As has already been stated, we do not know who they mostly were, or where they came from – perhaps from very far away indeed – but in all probability they had received something like a Greek education and training.

The imperial portraits that they produced were one of the outstanding creations of Roman art, and indeed of the art of the world at any and every time. They were truly magnificent, and undoubtedly played a great part in keeping the empire together. Imagine a world in which there was no television or radio: evidently the busts of the emperor fulfilled a comparable, essential role in binding all these disparate territories and peoples together. They had to be outstanding works of art in order to fulfil this purpose adequately. And that is what they were. From an artistic as well as a historical and political point of view they deserve our most careful study.

PORTRAITS OF PRIVATE INDIVIDUALS

The imperial portraits that have been discussed owed much to a long Roman tradition of private portraiture, and this was maintained during the principate, at many points in the empire. The earlier stage of the tradition, however, needs to be briefly discussed, so that we can see the former, historical background of the private portraits that continued to be made in various provinces as well as at Rome itself.

As was mentioned in the last chapter, portraiture was developed in the Hellenistic world, and this custom had been enlarged by the great families of republican Rome, who thus provide an essential chronological precedent for the Roman imperial portraits that have been discussed. This tradition arose because the minds of upper-class republican Romans had been strongly imbued with senses of factualism and history, and thus felt a strong attraction towards portrtaits which would perpetuate the features and expressions of individuals in whatever setting was appropriate to them and their careers – and without ignoring or neglecting their physical peculiarities. These Roman patrons, even more than the Greeks who had preceded them, looked for a sort of sculptural biography which recorded and summed up a man or woman's special characteristics only as keys to his or her achievements and experiences.

With such aims in mind, and Pliny the Elder testifies to the satisfaction that this practice caused,[1] these republican Romans had greatly expanded the art of portraiture, endowing it not only with purpose and financial backing, but also with a truly Roman purpose and dignity, and with a challenging, novel set of subjects – namely the resolute, craggy faces of themselves, and (in part imaginatively) of their ancestors: since the private and public memorials of the dead outnumbered those of the living.[2] These projects, and the features of their subjects, exhibit every conceivable blend between northern toughness and southern exuberance, just as the Romans, no doubt, did themselves.

Let us for a moment examine the specific social manifestations of this Roman interest in portraiture. For many years patricians had possessed the privilege of retaining in their homes, and parading at family funerals, the death-masks of their ancestors.[3] Portraits of dead men and women had already been seen on Etruscan funeral sarcophagi and urns since the third or second century BC, and the most vivid and lifelike of them, an alabaster commentary on matrimonial relations from Volaterrae (Volterra), is probably of the first century before our era.[4]

At Rome, where portraits had so frequently been of the dead, there was an increasing number of heads of the living as well. Evidence of Roman portrait-painting in Italy has almost completely disappeared (except for a few murals from Pompeii), but we are told that during the final period of the Roman republic, the Greek custom of putting up statues in honour of distinguished men spread to Rome, where senior functionaries became entitled to erect statues of themselves at central points of the city. This custom blended with the funerary tradition of the leading families to create a considerable demand for sculptural portraits. And that is the demand which the busts and images of the first century BC were intended to satisfy, and which led to the intense interest in expression and characterization that they manifest. The result was one of the principal glories of Roman civilization – portraits of private individuals as well as, later, of emperors, as we saw in the last chapter – and it was a glory that spread throughout the Roman empire.

But who, one must ask again, in republican as in later times, were the artists? Some of them were Romans, but probably this was not very frequently the case. Most of them, it may be repeated, were Greeks, or easterners whose upbringing, training and culture were Greek. Rome supplied the market, the money and many of the faces, and the artists came, as they had come in previous centuries, from the coastal districts facing the eastern Mediterranean and Aegean Seas. But these sculptors did not, usually, attain any lofty social status or position. Like other artists, they had risen in reputation under the Hellenistic monarchies, which permitted them a small fraction of the glory that their works were able to bestow upon those whom they depicted. But they remained, on the whole, at a social level beneath, say, that of architects, and nearer to tradesmen than to senators or senior functionaries of the state.

That is to say, although arguments to the contrary have been brought forward, it does not appear that the profession of sculptor attracted a notable number of educated Romans, or, for that matter, of educated Greeks, within the Roman empire.[5] The achievement of the sculptors, indeed, was prompted by Rome, and yet it was non-Romans and easterners who seem to have done most of the important work.[6] To take a particular instance, the carving of marble, utilized for sculpture in Roman homes (as well as for the decoration of their walls) from the first century BC onwards, required technical skills in which no one but those trained in near-eastern expertise were adequately versed.

Immigrants able to provide these skills, it can be said again, found extensive and well-paid employment at Rome, and their style, at its best, seems to have attained a truly international uniformity in which their origins were submerged. True, as we shall see, local schools elsewhere retained elements of their own traditions, which we can still recognize today. But the output of important sculptural schools within the central Greco-Roman region is sometimes not so easy to disentangle from the remaining portions of the imperial sculpture of the time, of which, indeed, it constituted an essential part.

However, one cannot fail to notice a considerable regional diversity of portrait styles. And yet, although the regions possess artistic features of their own, it is hard to pin them down, partly because most of the schools of sculpture throughout the Roman empire appear to have possessed the capacity to veer, at short notice, from archaic to classical styles, and from sentimentality (or elegant rococo) to realistic depictions of quite a brutal kind. Such changes, it would seem, may often have been due to the influence of some single individual, though it is impossible for ourselves, at this distance, to know who he or she was.

Out of these various styles the most typical of those that came to the fore in Rome during the first century BC possessed a characteristic that has been defined as *verism*. This is a somewhat dry form of realism, in which the subjects are depicted, as far as possible, as they actually are, without idealizing their physical appearance, and are portrayed not as poets or philosophers or visionaries but rather as men and women who lived an everyday life. The later Greeks had introduced an energetic style which was the predecessor or initial stage of this veristic approach. Influenced also by Etruscan castings of bronze, and possibly by Egyptian traditions as well, the opportunities that were now apparent in republican and then imperial Rome enabled portraiture to achieve an unprecedented development there.

During the years that had elapsed since the time of Alexander III the Great, the Greeks had developed further portrait styles as well, notably one laying emphasis upon emotional pathos, and others repeating the wholly idealistic tendencies of earlier epochs. But although manifestations of these styles were at times perceptible in republican Rome as well, they did not make a great deal of headway there. Verism rather than pathos or idealistic portrayals was what, in that tough age of individualism transformed into violence, the principal Romans required. And their Greek and Asian and other artists, as they sought to satisfy this requirement, duly affected Roman taste, both educating it and freeing it from more local, parochial influences, or at any rate modifying these by more universal tendencies.

When the principate came, under Augustus (31 BC–AD 14), private portraiture continued to flourish, together with the obviously novel custom of portraying emperors and their families, which was discussed in the last chapter. Indeed, from this time onwards, private portraiture flourished in almost every part of the empire. Innumerable examples could be cited from a variety of provinces. In the west, reference can be made to the number of private patrons whose portraits were included among more than seventy marble heads and busts found at the great Gallo-Roman villa at Chiragan near Toulouse;[7] and farther east, near the River Rhenus (Rhine), there was a rich range of private portraits, by artists of the most varied ethnic origins.[8] In Britain, such busts are fewer, but they have benefited from J. M. C. Toynbee's discussion of these objects and their origins, whether they came from Rome – or had been imported from elsewhere – or are local.[9] A small white marble head in the British Museum, if truly discovered at Blackheath near Camulodunum (Colchester), is, she remarks, an imported work of purely Roman style. Two Lullingstone busts probably 'represent part of the family portrait gallery of some individual in the imperial service, stationed in Britain for a longish term ... brought by him into the province'. But in the portrait of a Flavian lady at Aquae Sulis (Bath), likely to be a private person, 'the abnormally large, wide-open and rather staring eyes seem to betray the hand of a provincial carver'. And a head found at Hawkshaw in Peeblesshire, now in the National Museum of Antiquities of Scotland in Edinburgh, was 'probably worked in Britain in foreign marble imported for the purpose. The sculptor would seem to have been in some way associated with the army, a man well trained in Mediterranean iconographic traditions, but possibly betraying in his treatment of the hair a Gaulish origin.' Furthermore, heads in the Gloucester and Winchester Museums show fusions of classical and Celtic traits.

But the finest and most extensive non-imperial portraits come from the other extremity of the empire, where a flourishing sculptural school – not the only one in the east[10] – existed at Palmyra (Tadmor) on the Euphrates. Technically within the Roman province of Syria, although more or less independent, Palmyra is located at a crossroads, the southerly route leading to Mesopotamia. An oasis surrounded by the desert, of whose ways its citizens had direct experience, it was a staging-point for communications between the two countries, so that the Palmyrenes were, by nature, the middlemen and controllers of the caravan-routes which converged upon their city and met and crossed there, and which gave them – largely by virtue of their eastern trade – outstanding prosperity.[11]

The tall, rock-cut tower-tombs lining the approaches to the city, some of them five storeys high, testify to this wealth of the leading families of Palmyra. The superb funerary art, exemplified by fine busts, that these tombs contained, makes each grim tower with its small windows not merely a fortress where corpses might be laid but also a sort of apartment-house where the dead might dwell for eternity. This is an art which successfully brings together the multiple themes and forms of contemporary styles, and which displays an intriguing mixture of Roman and eastern manners.[12] For despite a general Greco-Roman framework, the physical types that these Palmyrene busts reproduce are eastern. The men's clothing is partly of that origin. The statues of the ladies of Palmyra, revealing their rank, are loaded with jewellery and enriched by resplendent headbands (Figure 4). These women wear fairly plain robes, it is true, which give a Greek impression, but the veils or head-dresses which so many of them display over their heads, not to speak of their features, are eastern in feeling.[13] 'The competent matrons', suggested Robin Fedden,

> set, responsible and provident, emerge as ... a salient type. They evidently

Figure 4 Portrait-bust of an entirely unknown leading citizen of Palmyra (Tadmor) in Syria.

The sculptors of the Roman empire excelled in the production of portraits not only of emperors and their families but of private citizens (as in the later republic), and in many parts of the empire these were skilfully carried out in accordance with local traditions, amended, very often, by some admixture of Greco-Roman influences. Palmyra's wealth, derived from east-west trade, was reflected in the excellent busts of dead leading citizens and their families in the unique tower-tombs on the outskirts of that city. The importance of women among these busts indicates their local social position.

18

do not underrate the new position and security which wealth has brought to the daughters of women who had once moved with tents and knew little more oasis comforts than beasts. Nothing in this civilisation is more extraordinary than these solemn, bejewelled matrons . . . who flourished for a few generations with the inhospitable sand blowing about the doors of their orderly houses.[14]

The passion for exactitude [observed I. A. Richmond] revealed in these vivid memorials of the dead vies with that of any funerary art in the west. No Roman millionaire could have been more set upon perpetuating his very self than these desert aristocrats, whose pride in achievement and zest for life proclaims itself in the care for minutest details.[15]

They disturb one, these Palmyrene portraits [writes Richard Stoneman]. Male and female alike stare out at you with an unsettling self-assurance, indeed an arrogance, not with a gaze that betokens anger at the disturbance of their rest but with a gaze fixed with absolute confidence on a beyond of whose lineaments we have absolutely no idea. The faces are sharply individual, and yet it is argued that all cannot be portraits in our sense, for in a few cases the same features reappear with different names attached. Yet we feel we know something of these haughty people clad in rich garments and jewelry and often accompanied by symbols that tell us more of their profession: the priest in his hat or diadem, the cameleer with a camel peering over his shoulder. It is inconceivable to me that these effigies should not be intended for portraits. . . . After all, such portraits are bound to be idealized: the subject did not sit on his death-bed for his portrait but commissioned it long before, so a man who died at seventy may well be represented by a portrait of a man of thirty-five.[16]

The upper storeys of the towers were sometimes sold to other tenants. One notable tomb is that of Elahbel, Manna, Shokadji and Malikhu, the four sons of Wahballath.[17] This tower, erected in April AD 103, rises up from a low, rock-cut ground floor to three further floors, presenting slit windows to the outside world. The statues of the four men, reclining upon richly carved and upholstered couches, exhibit a tranquil hauteur, and they look self-sufficient and self-satisfied. Below some of the couches are attendant grooms and pages. There are also winged djinns, who perhaps afforded protection in the journey to the beyond. Busts of relations are also to be seen; and others are to be found in the upper chambers.

There is a curious mixture, here, of various cultural elements, as has already been suggested for Palmyra in general terms. The influences of Rome and Greece are not lacking; but the general impression is scarcely Greco-Roman.

And how far are these heads entitled to be called portraits? A certain suspicion is raised by their repeated frontality. They are repetitive pieces of decoration, intricately patterned, with no distinctions or particularities of feeling about the large oval eyes of their subjects. They are not highly individualistic; they foreshadow the hieratic figures of future Byzantium. And yet what Stoneman says still remains valid: portraits they surely are, even if somewhat idealized, as portraits so often have to be.

*   *   *

Such portrait-busts which commemorate not the emperors of the Roman empire or members of their families, but private citizens, have an interest all of their own. In some cases, naturally enough, despite the long tradition of private portraits behind them, their very existence is due to the imperial heads, of which they are a kind of offshoot, but in other cases, notably (as we have seen) at Palmyra, they enjoy a life of their own, which illustrates the existence of local artistic achievements and traditions that owe at least as much, or more, to influences that are not Roman at all. In a number of regions these achievements and traditions are strong, bearing witness to an artistic life which was, in origin, independent of Rome, although it may often have been stimulated and invigorated by the Roman powerhouse and the artists the Romans attracted.

3

IMPERIAL RELIEFS

The Romans and the peoples who inhabited their empire were addicted to relief sculptures, because they were interested in compositions and subjects, more so, in fact, than in the details of the human body. There were quite a lot of relief sculptures at Palmyra, and more still at Aphrodisias, notably in the Sebasteion, a monumental zone dedicated to the cult of Augustus (in Greek, Sebastos) and his deified successors.[1] Some of these reliefs at Aphrodisias were mythological and backward-looking, since the Aphrodisians often went back to the mythical past, but certain of their other reliefs adopted a directly imperial subject-matter. Thus there were reliefs of Augustus himself, nude, accepting the bounties of the earth and command of the sea, and of

> other Julio-Claudian emperors, princes and princesses, crowning trophies and conquering nations. . . . Fortunately several of the imperial panels were identified by inscriptions. . . . Thus one showed Claudius overwhelming Britannia, another Nero conquering Armenia, and a third Rome receiving the bounties of the earth (Ge). The Nero relief, as well as a few other ones, betrayed intentional damage, including erasure of the emperor's name, obviously signs of *damnatio memoriae* [official posthumous condemnation].
>
> Over the years, the number of sculptors the city produced was very large. For lately, not only has new evidence emerged for Aphrodisias artists already known, but also many additions have been made to the twenty known signatures, notably Alexander the son of Zeno, Apollonius Aster and Menodotus. And there must surely be more names and works of art to come. Meanwhile, the sector of the town in which these men worked has been discovered, revealing trial pieces, unfinished works, rejects and tools.[2]

A large part of the sculptures which these men of Aphrodisias created consisted of reliefs, of which many were of this imperial character.

THE TROPHY OF TRAJAN

Work in this medium was, of course, very well known at Rome itself, where abundant reliefs are still to be seen; those on the Columns of Trajan and Marcus Aurelius are especially famous. But what is highly relevant to the imperial, provincial themes of this book is a sort of regionalized, amended echo of the former of these columns in faraway Dacia (Rumania), which the generals of Trajan (AD 98–117) had overrun and annexed to the empire, thus avenging the loss of many Roman soldiers near Tapae in the time of Domitian (88).

This monument, the Trophy of Trajan (Tropaeum Trajani), set up in AD 109, is a huge concrete drum, 100 feet in diameter,[3] 100 yards west of an altar and mausoleum (cenotaph) in honour of those Romans who had fallen while fighting against the Dacians in Domitian's time. The trophy was formerly erected upon a nine-stepped platform, and was dedicated to Mars Ultor (Mars the Avenger).

The drum of the monument was mainly decorated by a massive frieze, consisting of fifty-four panels – a pair for each theme – depicting Roman military operations by Trajan's army in the region of the Lower Danube (Figure 5). Above the cornice of the drum was a parapet, displaying the figures of prisoners of war, and behind the parapet rose a conical roof, surmounted by a two-storey hexagonal pedestal, from which rose the trophy itself, nearly 33 feet high, with three captives at its feet.

This is one of the most arresting monuments in the Roman empire, and offers unique testimony to the army and its foes. But it is also of particular interest because of the starkly, crudely provincial character of its reliefs. True, they deal with a Roman imperialistic theme, the conquest of Dacia, and in this respect they closely echo Trajan's Column at Rome. Yet the style of this Tropaeum Trajani is emphatically un-Roman, and the artist of these grim, terrifying reliefs was surely a Dacian.[4]

AN EMPIRE OF MANY NATIONS

The Romans, and the peoples of their empire, as we saw at the outset of this chapter, were interested in relief sculpture, because they liked viewing the action which this type of sculpture went in for. In particular, the imperial government saw reliefs as a potent means of celebrating its achievements. But it did not necessarily employ Romans or Italians to do so, even at Rome itself. For it seems probable that even the Column of Trajan in the capital was designed, or its design was supervised, by a Syrian or a Greek, Apollodorus of Damascus.

And what is also interesting is the hold that this form of art took in the provinces, where there were local or itinerant sculptors.[5] This chapter has recorded a number of such reliefs at Aphrodisias in Caria, and it is clear that the artists who celebrated the local conquests of Trajan at Tropaeum Trajani (Adamklissi) in Rumania were not Romans but provincials, whose non-Roman

Figure 5 Relief celebrating the victory of Trajan (AD 98–117) over the Dacians, and the annexation of their country, upon the Tropaeum Trajani at Adamklissi in Dacia (Rumania).

Just occasionally works of art in the Roman provinces seem quite uninfluenced by the pervasive Greco-Roman traditions. One such example is the reliefs on the Trophy of Trajan (Tropaeum Trajani) at Adamklissi – although the theme is entirely imperial: the victory of Trajan over the Dacians, whose country he annexed early in the second century AD. The victory was celebrated by thoroughly Greco-Roman reliefs on the Column of Trajan at Rome. But at Adamklissi a Dacian sculptor or sculptors brought to the task a strong measure of local taste and talent, producing masterpieces which are out of keeping with the dominant classical styles.

origin, as we have seen, emerges indubitably from the style of their reliefs, which is quite different from that of the columns at Rome. Thus the reliefs on the Adamklissi monument strike a powerful note in the symphony of the many nations that made up the Roman empire, and in various ways contributed to its art.[6]

4

SARCOPHAGI

The most remarkable and widespread repository for reliefs was the sarcophagus. What started this fashion was the gradual replacement of cremation by inhumation in the second century AD. Why this happened has been much discussed, but that it happened is certain. And in due course the preference for inhumation spread to the most distant provinces.

The result was the creation of prestigious, costly coffins, sarcophagi, which were constructed not only at Rome and Ostia[1] but also at Athens, and were also made beside sculptural quarries such as those at Aphrodisias and other centres of Asia Minor. In keeping with these varied origins, the sarcophagi also assumed a number of different shapes. There was an Attic form, an Asiatic form,[2] and a Roman or western form. The Attic and other eastern sarcophagus styles prolonged and perpetuated classicism in the sculpture of the third century AD. The decoration of the Asiatic columnar sarcophagi displays deep drilling and sharp outlines. All sarcophagi stress allegorical, mystical mythology, but perhaps those in the west most of all. They also show a restless interest in battles and hunting.[3]

In the history of art, these sarcophagi became increasingly predominant, replacing and superseding other artistic forms, and attracting the talents of the best Roman, Greek and eastern craftsmen and artists of successive imperial generations, who made such burial monuments the principal vehicles for sculptural ornament and pattern-making. This sort of relief sculpture attained excellence in the time of Hadrian (AD 117–38), and thereafter continued to grow rapidly. In Greece and Asia Minor, from a slightly later date, a number of independent workshops were producing sarcophagi for the Roman market.[4] In the history of all branches of Roman sculpture, the sarcophagi play a role of major significance – even if artistic masterpieces of the first quality are rare.

In general these reliefs bear eloquent witness to a widespread longing for salvation. The sarcophagi stress a spiritualized, non-terrestrial possibility of eternity. In the 'philosopher sarcophagi' this other-worldly aim is obvious: we are in the realm of higher values. But even the battle and hunting pictures display allegorical undertones of victory after death. And the mystical implications

Figure 6 The 'Temple' Sarcophagus found at Velitrae (Velletri) in Latium (Lazio). Third quarter of second century AD. Museo Civico, Velletri.

During the second century AD the replacement of cremation of the dead by inhumation led to a major amendment in artistic customs, for the sarcophagus now came into its own. And sarcophagi were covered with elaborate schemes of decoration which varied from region to region and became known by regional appellations. This third-century sarcophagus, discovered in 1955, seems to embody a mixture of the decorative schemes of different areas. One wonders who designed and made it, where he came from, and whether the sarcophagus itself was imported or made locally.

of the mythological scenes point in the same direction. 'Most people hoped for better times in the life to come.'[5]

Many of these themes of diverse geographical origin are apparent on a sarcophagus discovered some forty years ago at Velitrae (Velletri) south of Rome[6] (Figure 6) and now in the Antiquarium at Velletri. Crudely but fussily carved during the third quarter of the second century AD, it is a highly elaborate affair. The upper zone of the reliefs displays the Labours of Hercules – which symbolized the earthly life of human beings – between caryatids (female figures used as pillars) who supported an entablature which was crowned by a pediment, displaying Sol and Luna and other deities. The lower zone depicts scenes of torment in the underworld – showing the Danaids, Sisyphus, etc. – between figures of Titans.

And Proserpina is also to be seen, with Pluto. Her myth, including the descent through the gates of Hades and the eventual return, conveys the message of the translation of the soul towards its ultimate rejuvenation. For like so many of its counterparts this sarcophagus at Velitrae stresses the certainty of final victory and salvation after death. Its whole subject-matter proclaims the theatre of life and of death, echoing the characteristics of a theatre stage. Amid a spate of abstruse and somewhat confused imagery, the dead man, or the artist responsible for his sarcophagus, seems to want to introduce all the gods and heroes and cults imaginable in order to convey a message and further a cause.

This Velitrae monument is so large and heavy that it could not easily have been transported from abroad. So it was presumably made in Italy – and indeed that is what certain features of its style and decoration would lead us to suppose.[7] Yet it has a great deal in common with the 'Asiatic' type of sarcophagus, and suggests the employment of eastern models. That is to say, the Velitrae sarcophagus bears witness to the mobility of regional artistic trends, in the Roman empire. Very often, it is Roman influences that travel to the east. But here it is eastern tendencies – in the hands, no doubt, of immigrants from countries east of the Aegean – that have made their way to Italy.

*   *   *

Sarcophagi, as we have seen, became the principal medium of the sculpture and relief sculpture of the Roman empire. This was largely, we know, because the eyes and hearts of its peoples turned increasingly to thoughts of spirituality and the afterlife, so that themes had to be selected which responded to this taste and interest. Moreover, the process was facilitated by the love of reliefs which had made itself felt throughout the empire, as the previous chapter showed. And the sarcophagi particularly illustrate the international character of that empire, because they are found in many of its provinces, and adopt shapes and themes corresponding to local artistic and spiritual preferences. They are, in fact, a significant element in the internationalism and regionalism which were such notable features of that vast Roman world.

Part II

ARCHITECTURE

INTRODUCTION:
ARCHITECTURE AS AN ART

Ludwig Friedländer observed:

> Architecture is the only art in which the Romans showed any creative
> activity. Corresponding as it were to a national taste, it was the only art
> which could not only effectively promote the ambitious aims of the state
> and its universal dominion, but also adequately expressed the conscious-
> ness of its right to the empire of the world. While dependent upon Greek
> influence in all other departments of art, in architecture the Romans have
> created those absolutely original works which, in spite of thousands of
> years, even at the present day produce an effect so powerful and 'almost
> stupefying'[1] – works with which Greek art has nothing to compare. . . .
> The absolute necessity and the high importance of architecture in public
> as well as private life explains why it was considered the most respect-
> able of all arts. . . . Probably it was the most lucrative art not only in
> Rome but in all the large cities of the empire, and consequently
> overcrowded. In the ranks of architects Roman citizens were found by
> the side of slaves, freedmen and foreigners in Republican as well as
> Imperial times.[2]

Most of what Friedländer said there has stood the test of time. But his first
sentence must now be queried: imperial portrait sculpture, too, as we have seen,
could on occasion be excellent. And, even if architecture was regarded as
superior to the other arts – of all of which, indeed, Vitruvius maintained that
the architect should be the master[3] – I doubt if its practitioners were always so
well regarded, a good many of them being Greeks and easterners.[4] Yet, by and
large, the Romans recognized that the architecture of their empire, whoever
created it, was a wonderful thing.

Possessing a national ability to borrow, they improved and reshaped their
Greek and Etruscan prototypes. True, the people of the Roman empire, who
built for use and permanence and massive grandeur and extravagant, conspicuous consumption, were primarily concerned to make sensible or impressive
rather than beautiful architecture. But it is remarkable, nevertheless, to what an
extent this architecture of theirs engendered beauty as well. And indeed one of

the three principal requisites for the successful prosecution of this building activity laid down by Vitruvius, in his *De Architectura*, was *venustas*, beauty.

And he is echoed, in the present century (against those who see architecture only as a science), by Le Corbusier and Nikolaus Pevsner. The former wrote: 'The architect, by his arrangement of forms, achieves an order which is a pure creation of the spirit. . . . It is then that we experience beauty.'[5] And what Pevsner said was this: 'The term architecture applies only to buildings designed with a view to aesthetic appeal.'[6]

For certainly the Romans regarded architecture as an art. And it was an art at which they excelled – partly because of their employment of concrete and the barrel-vault, but also because of their innate taste for construction. It is not fortuitous that the only Roman treatise on an art that has come down to us is about architecture, the treatise by Vitruvius that has already been mentioned.

It is also of interest, though once again difficult, to detect the interaction of Roman and non-Roman (Etruscan and Greek) elements in the architecture of the Roman empire. On the one hand, it has been maintained that there was the same basic system of architecture throughout the Roman world. But let us stress the word 'basic'; for within the borders of this admitted fundamental unity there was, in architecture as well as other arts, a great number of local variations. Moreover, even at Rome itself the architects were not always, or usually, Romans. We do not, for the most part, know their names. But we do happen to be told, as was mentioned earlier, that the architect of Trajan at Rome, and designer or supervisor of his column and basilica there, as well as the constructor of the same emperor's bridge over the Danube near Debrecen, was Apollodorus.[7] He came from Damascus, but wrote in Greek. That is to say, his education was Greek, though he himself may well have been a Syrian. These external origins needs to be borne in mind when we think of 'Roman' architecture, though it was, indeed, inspired by imperial Rome.

5

PAGAN TEMPLES

The art of the Roman empire produced significant variations and developments of the Greek temple, though controversy has raged concerning the origin of these variations, and to what extent, for example, they were due to Etruscan middlemen. In any case, the features of these Greek temples that really struck the Romans were their external peristyles, and they themselves introduced the innovation of extending the original porch colonnade all round a temple, front, back and sides. They also liked a deep porch and a high podium, which meant that they rather got away from the Greek two-dimensional idea.

Probably the most remarkable of all temple complexes in the Roman empire was the group of three temples at Heliopolis (Baalbek) in Syria (Figure 7).[1] This was a scheme based on a huge rectangular court, with a hexagonal forecourt, both artificially raised, and both built of hard local limestone. The columns were made of grey or red granite and porphyry, and the colouring of the walls was bright, without the need for any painted stucco. It would appear that the principal temple at Heliopolis was built in the middle of the first century AD, and that construction continued thereafter and was completed in the course of the third century, when an additional temple was added.

Two points about this complex deserve special attention. First, its enormous size was remarkable. One of the principal achievements of the Roman empire was not only the reshaping but the enlargement and aggrandizement of the Greek tradition, and Wheeler has argued that this aggrandizement was a creative, artistic feat in itself.[2] Its purpose at Heliopolis was to impress easterners with Roman magnificence – with the power of Roman rule in Syria. And it achieved this aim by a judicious blend of Roman, Greek and eastern influences. The blend is symbolized by the triad of deities who were worshipped at this centre: they are Jupiter, who is the eastern Baal, and Venus, who is the Syrian Atargatis, and Mercury, who was no doubt likewise assimilated to some eastern, non-Greco-Roman counterpart. And in the process of assimilation the temples borrow their structure and their rich decoration from Rome, and yet they also retain local elements, including two towers of eastern derivation: so that the scheme, by this means, symbolizes the perpetuation of a native

Figure 7 Reconstruction of the temples of Jupiter (Baal) and other deities at Heliopolis (Baalbek) in Syria. First to third centuries AD.

Roman utilization of concrete created monuments that had earlier been inconceivable, among them the temples which were the outward, public expression of ancient paganism. These, of course, were built not only in Rome – where we hear of an eminent architect (Apollodorus) from Damascus – but in many other regions of the Roman world as well. The huge religious complex at Heliopolis, a conspicuous example, is also a tribute to the multicultural character of imperial architecture: because although the complex was based upon, and derived from, the local shrine of a non-Roman, Semitic cult, its re-creation in Roman imperial times was conducted in Greco-Roman architectural terms, modified by local requirements and (no doubt) local architects and artists.

megalithic tradition. Here is the mixture of traditions that constituted the art of the Roman empire at its most impressive.

In other words, pagan temples erected in the provinces amalgamate Roman influences with those inherited from their own regional pasts. These were heady unions, which contributed to the readiness of all these peoples to accept and even welcome the reality of the Roman conquest. And the Romans, no doubt abetted by artists and architects who were not of Roman origin, responded by actively and willingly incorporating local brands of paganism into their own imperial religion, and into the art which sprang from that religion.

6

HOUSES

But it was not only imposing public vastness at which people in the Roman empire excelled. They also built interesting private houses. Admittedly some of the tenements in the cities were deplorable, but the accident of the eruption of Mount Vesuvius in AD 79 has shown us extraordinary examples of private (if gracious) living, at Pompeii and Herculaneum and Stabiae, illustrating the fact that Roman art, for all its temples, is primarily unreligious, an art of organized humanity.[1] It also represents a considerable element of artistic achievement. Much of this excellence was to be found in the provinces. But it is to the cities of Campania that we must preferably turn, because owing to the Vesuvius eruption they are so much better preserved.

THE HOUSES OF POMPEII AND HERCULANEUM

The eruption of Vesuvius

> which overwhelmed and thus partly preserved commercial Pompeii and residential Herculaneum, has . . . made it possible to reconstruct the main features of the houses. . . . [They] were perhaps not unlike those of well-to-do Greeks of the preceding epochs. But there is one apparently un-Greek feature, the long and lofty *atrium*. Half court and half front-room, containing the family altar and the ancestral statues, this, together with parts of the room beyond, could be glimpsed as one entered the front door. At the other end of the *atrium* was the peristyle, the centre of the private part of the building, surrounded by bedrooms, reception rooms, kitchens and dining rooms – usually made to accommodate nine people, and including rooms with different aspects for summer and winter. The peristyle sometimes contained a small garden, but on larger properties the garden lay beyond.
>
> These dwellings at Pompeii and Herculaneum presented plain façades to the street; and when the towns had begun to go down in the world, if not before, the frontage on either side of the entrance was let off as shops. The absence of windows towards the street – as in Arab houses of old

Cairo – was probably for the sake of privacy; glazed windows, though known, were little used. The rooms were lit by openings on internal courts, but except in the peristyle these were not large, since the sun was often strong – the house was heated by braziers when it was cold.

In some houses at Pompeii, and more at Herculaneum, there seem to have been upper floors, to which the domestic water supply, when it existed, was carried by leaden pipes. These upper floors were made of timber which, painted and gilded, was also used for the ground-floor ceilings.[2]

The houses were entered by a narrow corridor divided by a door into two successive halves, first the *fauces* and then the *vestibulum*. Next, according to the traditional plan, comes the court or *atrium*, usually with a central opening in its roof, situated over a basin to collect the rain-water. . . . On either side of the *atrium*, normally at its far end, were rooms called wings (*alae*). . . . The room known as the *tablinum*, behind the *atrium* in the centre, was closed at the back by a wall containing a door or window. . . . Like the bedrooms of the houses, the dining-room (*triclinium*) could be in a number of different places. . . . Kitchen arrangements were makeshift and cramped. . . . The Hellenistic taste for colonnades and porticoes [was] adapted to Italian needs. Some rich residences . . . had two, or even more, of these colonnaded peristyles. . . . Sometimes, too, the garden broke right outside the bounds of the colonnaded courtyard. . . . The luxury of water and plants was rated very highly indeed, and this passion explains a great deal in Roman architecture and art.[3]

The so-called 'House of Pansa' at Pompeii[4] (Figure 8) is a particularly grand and regular classical example of this kind of building. It occupies, together with its garden, an entire *insula*, or block. Nothing remains of the decoration. Constructed at an early date for a single family, it was subsequently divided up along its west and east sides into a number of apartments which were let out to tenants, with separate entrances of their own from several streets. The original nucleus of the house is represented by an *atrium* with adjoining *alae* and *tablinum* and by a peristyle, in the centre of which stands a large tank or pool instead of the customary garden. At the furthest extremity of the peristyle there is a big hall, and on the left a kitchen, a stable with a latrine, and a room that served as a shed (in which carts could be kept). Behind these premises another wing opens out into an extensive garden area, which is now a plant-nursery.

The 'House of Pansa' was designed for a single family, perhaps the Arriani Polliani; its last proprietor was Marcus Nigidius Vaccula, whose name has survived from an election notice. It is now becoming fashionable to consider the social (as well as medical) positions of those who dwelt in these houses, particularly if they or their immediate forebears were immigrants. For this seems to have been a mobile (although hierarchical) society, in which the

Figure 8 A prosperous house of the first century AD at Pompeii overwhelmed by the eruption of Mount Vesuvius in AD 79: the House of Pansa, looking through the *atrium* to the colonnaded garden court (peristyle) and to Mount Vesuvius beyond.

These houses adopted variations of a general plan based on ground-floor extensions round a central *atrium*, beyond which was the *tablinum* (a room of traditional character), the *triclinium* (dining-room) and, very often, as here, a colonnaded garden. Intended for prosperous people, they contained elaborate wall-paintings and floor mosaics.

expensive development of such houses played a part in enabling their owners to establish themselves as Romans, and Romans of a fairly distinguished kind.

THE TENEMENTS IN OSTIA

In the second century AD (and indeed earlier), in contrast to and reaction against these costly dwellings, tenement building, which had been of such dubious quality before, was improved, and to this development Rome's port of Ostia bears witness; for it is there that the most abundant archaeological evidence for such tenements is still extant. Nearly eighty house-blocks (*insulae*) have now been identified, including 364 structures and 205 apartment houses[5] (Figure 9); and now no doubt more are coming to light.

Figure 9 Reconstruction of a five-storey tenement building at Ostia, the port of Rome, occupying a block (*insula*) in the residential part of the town. Early second century AD.

As the imperial epoch developed, it became clear that the traditional type of house at Pompeii, extending horizontally, occupied too much space, and cost too much as well. Tenement-buildings were therefore erected at Ostia, improving on the sinister slum constructions which had attracted unfavourable comment at Rome.

The exteriors of these buildings generally presented a functional appearance (in final rejection of the Greek stone heritage). Usually, they were constructed of unfaced brick. However, façades could be vaulted. And while the architects avoided the closed form of house familiar at Pompeii, the arches and window-lintels of the Ostia buildings (like their doors and walls and ceilings) might be brightened up by the application of red paint. And another sort of decoration could be provided by pillars or pilasters at the entrance.

There were also, in some of the blocks, built-out balconies, resting upon projecting wooden beams or corbels of stone or concrete, or, less frequently, brick. And in some cases these balconies must have been entirely ornamental and non-functional, since they sometimes, rather curiously, do not correspond with storeys and floors. The apartments inside these blocks were reached from courtyards, or by staircases coming upwards from the street in between an otherwise continuous line of shops. For most of the Ostian apartment blocks incorporated such shops at ground-floor level, sometimes behind a portico.

A recurrent apartment plan consists of five or six rooms served by a broad corridor which overlooked the street. The last of these rooms (the *medianum*) was usually much larger than the others, and there were often two other flanking rooms (*exedrae*). Regular rows of windows, facing on to the street or on to a garden or inner court, provided light and air, making the apartments less inward-looking and introspective than the old Pompeian houses.

Tenants were able to enjoy a fair measure of comfort, although no provision was made for private sanitation or furnace heating; chimneys did not exist. But at least these high-rise apartments were not only roomy but quite compact, as well as fire-proof, and they were very often close to the centre of the town and its main streets, which was convenient since traffic was restricted. The largest blocks could accommodate more than a hundred tenants. They were designed to provide reasonably sound and secure lodging for middle-class as well as upper-class citizenry.

'This was the first great social architecture, showing how houses as well as public monuments could be constructed with dignity for the needs of almost all ranks [*sic*] of a great organized society.'[6]

HEROD THE GREAT'S PALACES AT MASADA

The emperor himself resided in a palace on the Palatine Hill in Rome, and client monarchs too, outside the imperial frontiers but dependent on the Romans, were permitted to build and dwell in palatial residences as rewards for their obedience. One king of this type, at the very beginning of the principate, was Herod the Great of Judaea (36–4 BC). He constructed a considerable number of palaces for himself, and among them were two at the southern, Idumaean end of the Dead Sea, which are unmatched by any within the frontiers of the Roman empire.

He built these two palaces at one and the same place, the bleakest and most desolate site possible, on the top of the hill of Masada (Figure 10).[7] 'Surely', says Palestine's geographer George Adam Smith about this Dead Sea desolation, 'there is no region of earth where Nature and History have so cruelly conspired, where so tragic a drama has obtained so awful a theatre.'[8] This huge, boat-shaped rock had been the refuge in which Herod lodged his family in 40 BC when the Parthians swept through the country, and he was hastening to Rome for support. But that association does not fully explain his choice of this location. There was also something in his own personality that recommended a location which was melodramatically remote from human contacts, amid a landscape so stricken and so fantastic that it is scarcely possible for a photograph to do it justice.

> The largest of his two Masada mansions covered thirty-six thousand square feet at the western extremity of the plateau. The numerous important finds . . . have included the throne room, and an entrance hall. [Mosaics abound.] A kitchen, too, has come to light . . . and store rooms. . . .
>
> Much stranger, however, was Herod's second palace at Masada, which stood at the narrow northern extremity of the same hill-top, and indeed jutted beyond it on three terraces, hanging, one above the other, right over the abyss, with the support of massive eighty-foot-high supporting walls. The lowest terrace, containing rooms and baths and pilastered, painted colonnades, was designed chiefly for enjoying the grim and startling scenery. This, too, was the purpose of the middle terrace, which included a decorative circular building. The upper terrace provided living accommodation for Herod and his most intimate entourage (the rest were accommodated elsewhere on the hill). . . . At the northern extremity, a large semi-circular portico commanded an amazing view on three sides of the compass. . . .
>
> Only a builder of the ambitions of Herod could have conceived the project of erecting a three-tiered hanging palace-villa for himself on this spot.[9]

Moreover Masada, like Herod's other chosen abodes, was to remain a fortress as well as a palace; and he rebuilt the great wall extending a mile round the precipitous hilltop.

Nobody, it has rightly been said, can visit this awesome spectacle without experiencing mixed emotions, including admiration for the engineering virtuosity of the palace builders.

As usual, we do not know who they were. But this, it has been rightly said, 'was late Hellenistic architecture with strong Italian overtones'[10] – imposed, with the utmost skill and flair, upon scenery which was alien to both traditions. Nevertheless, they are traditions which the palaces do not allow us to forget. For between the columns of a square building on the lowest terrace of the northern palace, painted plaster imitated a multicoloured, marble revetment – a

Figure 10 Masada, beside the Dead Sea: the palace of Rome's client-king Herod the Great of Judaea (36–4 BC).

Client-kingdoms, although technically independent, and left in control of internal affairs, were dependent in foreign and general policy on the rulers of the Roman empire. They contributed troops when necessary, in return for imperial support and friendship, and were permitted, very often, to construct stupendous palaces for themselves.

Herod was a great builder, and one of his most remarkable and peculiar constructions was the palace of Masada, perched on several levels of a lofty hill beside the Dead Sea. The palace demonstrates how the accumulated traditions of classical architecture could be woven into the idiosyncratic framework which the monarch required for himself.

style of decoration both popular in the Hellenistic East and reminiscent of the houses of the wealthy at Pompeii and elsewhere in Italy. And in the south-eastern corner of this lower terrace was a bath of the Roman type.

PIAZZA ARMERINA

These were the palaces of a king, even if he was a king dependent on Rome; and three centuries later the palace of a private citizen uniquely attained equal grandeur in Sicily, at Philosophiana near Piazza Armerina (Figure 11).[11] It has been conjectured that this huge residence was intended to house the Emperor Maximian, after his abdication accompanying the abdication of Diocletian (AD 305), who thereafter lived in his great palace at Spalatum, of which more will be said later. But although the date for Piazza Armerina seems to be right (despite debate), this conclusion is unlikely. The palace's mosaics, which are nowadays the most spectacular adornment of the buildings, dwell upon fights with wild beasts, and it seems probable that the owner of the residence was a private citizen who made his wealth by importing animals from Africa to fight in the amphitheatres of Italy and Sicily.

The residence at Piazza Armerina was constructed, for the most part, according to what was evidently a single, initial plan, although it may well be that one major modification (and certainly a number of minor ones) became introduced not long after the building was first put up. It was a single-storeyed edifice made throughout of mortared rubble, with facings consisting of pieces of brown stone quarried nearby. String-courses are limited to corners and other points of structural significance, where stone blocks were laid with particular care.

The main entrance to the mansion was a monumental triple archway, framed by Ionic columns and punctuated by niches, and further adorned by fountain basins. The entrance leads into a courtyard with another fountain basin in the centre, and a colonnade all round. From this courtyard visitors have to turn sharply to the right in order to reach the main part of the villa, and when they do so they walk through a spacious vestibule of rectangular shape, emerging into a central peristyle round which is grouped an extensive part of the villa's living quarters.

In the middle of the peristyle was a decorative pool, which was apparently in the centre of a garden. The peristyle, like the courtyard, is surrounded by a portico. Its columns are of granite and marble (including *cipollino*), and their capitals are Corinthian. The peristyle had ten columns along two of its sides and eight along the other two. At one of its corners is a bathing (thermal) establishment, a complex group of interlocking rooms set at an oblique angle to the main structure of the villa.

From the eastern extremity of the peristyle a stairway, comprising three flights of steps, leads up to a transverse corridor, over 200 feet in length, terminating at both ends in apses. There was also a large apsed hall, known as

Figure 11 The fourth-century house at Philosophiana (Piazza Armerina) in Sicily.

This mansion, in the centre of the island, apparently belonged to some rich private citizen, who probably obtained his wealth by importing wild animals from Africa and elsewhere to Italy and Sicily for slaughter in the arenas. Architecturally, the main interest of the mansion lies in its designer's deliberate rejection of classical symmetry. While retaining the outward signs of the Greco-Roman heritage, he has laid out a convoluted plan, involving unsymmetrical twists and turns.

the 'basilica', reached from the eastern side of the corridor. The hall was presumably intended for banquets and other such functions. And the owner of the house may have sat there to hear petitions from clients.

A southern apartment, containing impressive floors and planted round a small semicircular courtyard adorned with a fountain, may have been the suite in which the owner and his family lived. And there is a further apartment, too, in this southern part of the villa, consisting of three small chambers on either side of a larger, oval, colonnaded court. Decoration, especially in the form of mosaics, was abundant.[12]

So here we have an inorganic, curvilinear, twisting, restlessly convoluted, optically surprising aggregation of more or less independent groups of rooms, juxtaposed so as to show an avoidance of axiality and symmetry, a 'persistent deviousness, eternal changing of direction, and hiding of the goal'. Hidden in a lush, wooded, intimate valley, the house 'huddled in the landscape but ignored it'. The terrain is skilfully exploited, yet 'the old intimate association with the surrounding landscape has been lost, giving place to an inward-turning self-sufficiency'.[13]

DIOCLETIAN'S PALACE AT SPALATUM

Of about the same date is the very different but equally massive palace, villa, or château at Spalatum (Split, near Salonae in Dalmatia), built for the Emperor Diocletian who abdicated in AD 305 (Figure 12).

His residence there has survived on a far more impressive scale than any other. This was the project, supported by the appalling taxation of the time, upon which Diocletian spent the years of his retirement, outdoing the numerous palaces of his predecessors and younger colleagues and Persian rivals. This blend of civil and military architecture, much more compact than Piazza Armerina, amalgamated the public rooms of a palace, the residential quarters of a great Dalmatian villa or a commander-in-chief's house, and an inward-looking impregnable fortress, guarded by a wall that was studded by square and polygonal towers. Central to this ruthlessly axial plan is a main avenue which leads through the palace city up to the focal Hall of Audience. Beyond a colonnaded courtyard (*atrium*), the main surviving feature of this throne-room is its three-bayed columnar façade, crowned by a gabled Pediment of Glorification. Over the middle columns curves an arch, beneath which, as if framed by the vault of heaven, Diocletian made his appearances and received homage like a divine effigy. Behind the courtyard was a domed circular vestibule with four small apses, and behind that again the shrine-like Hall of Audience itself, where the retired, revered emperor sat, jewelled and haloed, beneath a columned canopy.

On either side of the courtyard approaching these buildings stand

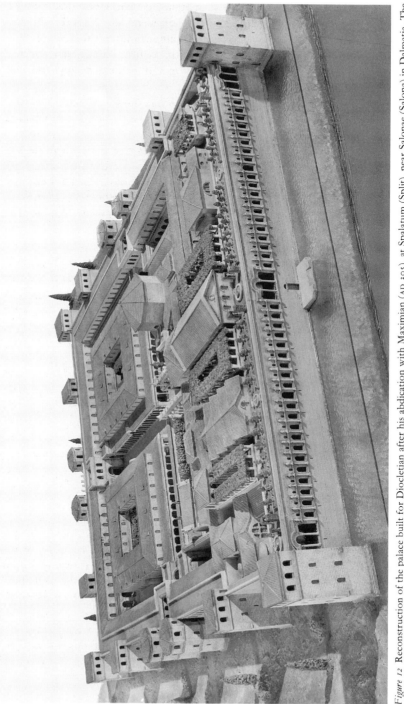

Figure 12 Reconstruction of the palace built for Diocletian after his abdication with Maximian (AD 305), at Spalatum (Split), near Salonae (Salona) in Dalmatia. The building is a combination of a magnificent country-house, a palace equipped with an imperial throne-room, and a fortress with strong defences. In view of these requirements it is designed symmetrically, on the lines of a military camp.

arcades of which the arches are not surmounted by horizontals but spring straight from the Corinthian columns in an energetic, un-classical fashion, which had occasionally been seen since Augustan times but was now fully exploited in the form which was to lead to the main architectural styles of later Europe. Another forward-looking type of colonnade appears on Salonae's richly decorated Golden Gate, which has a row of seven dummy arches like those at Shapur I's Ctesiphon. This gate, once flanked by towers, stands at the far north end of the processional avenue which leads through the town to the Hall of Audience at its opposite extremity. The south face of the Hall looked directly upon the sea, and here, between two square towers, the wall is broken by a gallery with a loggia at each end and in the centre. The gallery has forty-two arched windows; between them are engaged columns which rest upon blocks (corbels) projecting from the wall, above the north gate. This had happened before, but now the scale was more impressive.[14]

Here we have got right away from the defiance of axiality and symmetry which was so characteristic of Piazza Armerina. For Diocletian's palace, on the other hand, is a block of mathematical regularity, although some have pointed to certain departures from such rigidities which might be regarded as characteristic of an age in which there was a notable clash between mechanical co-ordination and free grouping.

The palace has a fortress-like form, so that instead of being merely a villa it is a fortified *castellum*, as is emphasized by the flanking towers, which are square and octagonal in shape. This military, fortress-like character was partially dictated by the general insecurity of the provinces during this unsettled period. But it was also, in part, motivated by Diocletian's fears for his own safety, which the configuration of his palace met as best it could.

But if he was insecure, he was also divine. His ceremonial suite became a sort of holy of holies, *palatium sacrum*, in which the former emperor was enthroned like a divine object of worship. In this concept, we see the idea of the mystery and seclusion which should envelop the person of the godlike Diocletian.

This is an eastern conception, and it is embodied in various eastern architectural features that go beyond the basic Roman military formulation. For example, the arch above the palace entrance is Syrian, and eastern influence is also made manifest in the arcaded portico on either flank of its forecourt, and in the arcade (in relief) carried on blocks (corbels) projecting from the wall above the north gate, and in the brick vaulting of the mausoleum (of which more will be said elsewhere). And the entire treatment of the Golden Gate (*Porta Aurea*) is characteristically Syrian. At the same time, however, there are other features in the construction that are equally typically occidental. Although sometimes described as tasteless, and conspicuously wasteful, this is a bold architectural plan, combining the elements of the two worlds with skill.[15]

7

PLACES OF ENTERTAINMENT

Places of entertainment were of a very varied character, which gave architects every opportunity to demonstrate their artistic skills.

THE LIBRARY OF CELSUS AT EPHESUS

Libraries were fully developed in imperial Rome, although no trace of them is now extant in the city. A good deal has survived, however, of the second-century library of Celsus at Ephesus (Selçuk) in Ionia (Figure 13).[1] Finished in AD 120–35, it had been dedicated by his son to the rich local citizen Tiberius Julius Celsus Polemaeanus, who had been consul at Rome (in AD 92) and was, unusually, buried within the city limits of Ephesus, in fact in a vaulted room below the library. Later heirs had completed the building.

Its interior was a high rectangular chamber, 55 feet wide and 36 feet long, with a small central apse, which stood above the tomb of Celsus. This apse was approached by a large arch, and presumably contained a statue – either of Celsus himself, or of Athena the patroness of wisdom and learning. Around three sides of the main hall there were rectangular pigeon-holes or niches, arranged in tiers, and containing cupboards or shelves in which the books were housed. Two of these tiers can still be seen, and originally there was a third, above them. This, and the tier immediately below it, could be reached from a gallery of horseshoe shape, furnished with balustrades, running round three sides of the hall, and supported by two sets of columns. This gallery was made accessible by stairs, which also extended downwards to the tomb of Celsus below. The walls of the library were thick enough to protect the books from damp. Its ceiling was flat, and may have had an open space in the centre.

The library stood on a platform. With the assistance of fragments discovered during the excavations, it has proved possible to reconstruct the façade of the building. Bases still to be seen in front of it suggest that it displayed four pairs of columns, which were given additional height by the pedestals on which they stood – a recent innovation with a long late antique and early Christian career ahead of it. Between the columns, there appear to have been three entrances to the building. They were evidently surmounted by windows, set into the second

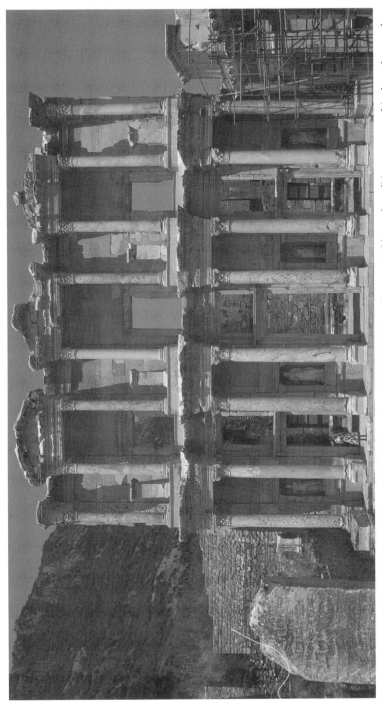

Figure 13 The Library of Celsus, at Ephesus (Selçuk) in Ionia (western Asia Minor), still in remarkably good condition, was erected in the early second century AD.

Public libraries for book-scrolls were built not only at Rome itself (now lost) from the beginning of the imperial epoch, but at other points throughout the empire. The extensive remains of the second-century Library of Celsus, in the Roman imperial province of Asia, give a good idea of what the libraries in the principal cities of the Roman world were like.

tier of the gallery. Carved and triangular pediments alternated, according to a widespread late Hellenistic formula that was now being given a new lease of life. People admired the well-planned unity and balance of this sort of elaborate façade, which aimed at a three-dimensional, undulating effect, and created an illusion of projecting and receding at one and the same time.[2]

THE BATHS AT AQUAE SULIS

The inhabitants of the Roman world were also enormously addicted to baths, of which they learned from Rome itself, since the capital city possessed a variety of such establishments.

Bath-buildings were habitually combined with structures and spaces devoted to other leisure activities: libraries, lecture-halls, lounges, sports grounds, gardens and paths for walks, all put together in a clever homogeneity and symmetry of design. The bath itself, however, retained its central position. Architects concerned with the planning of such sites set out to create an unrepetitive current of movement, incorporating a wide variety of shapes and sizes, without forgetting the economy of function that was basically required.

Throughout the western world this type of institution proliferated – not only in Rome itself, but notably in Spain. Quite early in the first century AD, in the speedily advancing communities of this Romanized country, baths formed an essential and inevitable part of public buildings. And a century later they proliferated in a wide variety of forms.

> One such complex comprised the Baths of La Reina Mora at Italica in Baetica, constructed while Hadrian was emperor (AD 117–38). This large assemblage of structures, measuring more than two hundred and thirty by a hundred and seventy feet, was made wholly of concrete, with specially manufactured bricks as facings. The arrangement of the rooms was symmetrical, based on an axis which extended from north-east to south-west, the principal architectural features being two adjoining, square, vaulted chambers opening onto a cold plunge-bath (*frigidarium*), which was nearly seventy feet long and terminated in an elegant apse. Adjacent was a spacious hall, with a nave, two aisles and a double colonnade. There was also a hot room (*caldarium*), and a gymnasium (*palaestra*). These Baths of La Reina Mora were lavishly decorated, with marble columns, painted wall plaster, stucco and mosaic floors, though little of all this ornamentation can be seen at the present time.[3]

Thamugadi (Timgad) in Libya, too, had no fewer than fourteen identified sets of bath buildings, bearing witness to the careful conservation of water which was characteristic of Africa.[4]

The Romans and local authorities, in such centres, were accustomed to build for use and perpetuity, and the massive magnificence of what they constructed was a perfect embodiment of the Roman taste for grandeur; so that such buildings were of considerable social significance.

> The Romans deserve the credit for combining the spiritual, social and therapeutic values of bathing and exalting it to an art. . . . Baths were the focus of communal life, offering a place for relaxation, social gathering and worship. . . . Caesars seeking popularity built *thermae* for their people and soon philanthropists followed, building their own elaborate baths as a sort of public relations gesture. Thus the bath-house evolved from a simple, wood-enclosed, single-function unit, small and austere, into a complex, luxurious, spacious, multi-functional establishment. . . . The intricate architectural layout of the *thermae* gave birth to an elaborate bathing ritual . . . the baths . . . promoted not only cleanliness but also an admiration for sports and culture.[5]

That is to say, there were facilities for a variety of sports as well as centres for reading and lectures.

Naturally enough, this high significance attached to the baths meant that attention was also paid to their potential artistic qualities, so that, indeed, they made an outstanding contribution to architectural design and planning.

Men, and increasingly women, spent a great deal of their time every day bathing and swimming in these thermal centres, and engaging in the various kinds of social life that were available there.[6] In order to satisfy the Romans' predilection for such activities, and their keen attention to the water supply which was so essential to this sort of activity, many of the baths at Rome and other centres were artificial, fed by water which was brought from elsewhere. But in other places, outside Rome itself, baths were created out of existing spas and springs.

Often they had started as sacred springs where people worshipped, and like similar sanctuaries in other provinces provided a remarkable, versatile blend of religious, curative and social welfare. This was notable in Roman Gaul, and in Britain, too; the thermal establishment at Bath (Aquae Sulis) (Figure 14) formed just such a complex, with many rooms containing spacious plunge-baths full of water that came direct from the springs and helped to counteract rheumatic and lymphatic illnesses. Bath, where Sulis Minerva was worshipped, was not a large town.[7] All the buildings inside the walls were eclipsed by the massive curative baths, the most imposing known in western Europe. This establishment, in so far as we can reconstruct it, seems to have been planned originally as three adjacent plunge-baths or swimming-baths, fed by a deep and abundant natural spring, of which the temperature reached 120° Fahrenheit; so that the establishment provided agreeable bathing in addition to its healing capacity.

> The steaming waters of Caer Baden thrilled the Romans when they arrived in AD 76. . . . The temple, the spa and the theatre formed the nucleus of a great social and spiritual centre that dominated the town for

Figure 14 The Roman bath at Aquae Sulis (Bath) in Britain. First century AD.

Some of the grandest baths have been partially preserved at Rome, but there were many variations throughout the provinces, some entirely artificial creations, others based on earlier springs, often hot, and often also dedicated to some local deity.

At Aquae Sulis, a sacred spring was developed into a famous and magnificent thermal establishment, of which the principal features can still be seen today.

four centuries. The King's Bath spring, in the centre of Bath, bubbles out of the ground at the rate of a quarter of a million gallons a day, maintaining a temperature, as we saw, of 46.5 degrees Celsius (120 degrees Fahrenheit). The source of its water is rain that fell about ten thousand years ago and penetrated deep into the earth, where it was warmed by the natural heat of the earth's core.

To the Romans the spring was not merely a source of hot water but a sacred place where mortals could communicate with the deities of the underworld. . . . An important function of the sacred spring was to bring retribution to one's enemy. If a person felt persecuted in some way . . . he/she would go to the temple scribe and compose a letter to the goddess . . . the Bath curses are extraordinary documents . . . giving us a glimpse into the hopes, expectations and piety of a society during four hundred years of Roman occupation. . . .

[In modern times] an excavating team discovered that the spring was contaminated with amoebic meningitis; it had to be cleaned out and all the pipes replaced . . . the baths remained closed for more than a decade; but now they are open once again.[8]

The largest of these thermal halls at Bath was the Great Bath itself, which was flanked by graceful porticoes with niches. Originally, the Great Bath possessed no overhead covering, but it subsequently obtained a roof, consisting of a vast tunnel vault, measuring some 35 feet across, with big open lunettes at either end, through which the steam could escape. This vault required that the piers of the colonnade should be considerably strengthened, and this was done.

The whole plan was ambitious and contained a high degree of luxury, as its ornate pediment suggests, as well as the figured panels which were both elegant and vigorous. Here was a project which brought the most sophisticated Roman architecture to Britain. And even to this day the hot water still gushes up and flows into the great swimming pool, through a massive conduit of Mendip lead.

THE THEATRE AT ASPENDUS

But the peoples of the Roman empire did not spend their whole leisure time in baths. They also demanded specific, dramatic entertainments. One was provided by the theatre, of which Aspendus (Belkis) in Pamphylia (southern Asia Minor) provides the finest surviving example (Figure 15).[9] Indeed, it is the best preserved of all ancient theatres, anywhere in the world. It was constructed in the second century AD by the architect Zeno, and presented to the community by two brothers.

The long, narrow backdrop (*scaenae frons*) of the Aspendus theatre, decorated with lavish ornamentation, has been amply preserved, and still stands as high as it originally was. This backdrop is pierced by five doors, above which are four rows of windows, varying one from another in shape and dimensions. And one,

Figure 15 The theatre at Aspendus (Belkis) in Pamphylia (southern Asia Minor), constructed in the second century AD by an architect named Zeno, who was presumably either a Greek or a local man with Greek education.

The Roman love of theatrical performances (at least less morally deplorable than their liking for gladiatorial shows) meant a widespread creation of new theatres, often rising straight off the ground rather than cut out of the rock as Greek theatres had so often been. One of the best-preserved theatres of the Roman imperial epoch is at Aspendus.

at least, of the doors was used to admit animals, when the theatre came to be employed for wild beast contests and shows. Above the top row of windows, and below it as well, projecting corbels can be seen, pierced with holes. These holes contained the ends of wooden masts, which held up an awning intended to shelter the spectators from the sun. The orchestra is semicircular, in the Roman manner – indeed Roman influence is perceptible elsewhere as well,[10] although it may not have been a Roman who constructed the theatre. The stage, which projected some 23 feet out from the backdrop, was apparently covered by a sloping wooden roof.

The whole building shows high standards of construction – and a massive scale of expenditure.

THE AMPHITHEATRE AT NEMAUSUS

There was, as we have seen, a certain amount of slaughter of animals in the theatre at Aspendus. But the men and women of the empire – especially in the west – wanted more of this sort of thing than a mere theatre could provide for them, that is to say, buildings especially adapted for this purpose: and adapted, also, to the slaughter of men by other men.

We today, from a moral point of view, find it difficult to appreciate, by way of contrast, the finer aspects of Roman civilization, given the appalling love of its peoples for the slaughter of gladiators and wild animals. There is no avoiding the fact that public slaughter, for the Romans, was an essential institution. If one had to defend it, one could say that it 'inspired a glory in wounds and a contempt for death'.[11] But that, to our minds, is unconvincing special pleading. All the same, this slaughter did provide lessons regarding pain and death, and regarding the fragility of life. It was a horrifying demonstration of the fates which could befall those who did not manage to please their masters. It was institutionalized terror such as was never seen again, until twentieth-century dictatorships, backed by modern technological resources, made it practicable to instil terror with even greater efficiency.

We can only sum up by concluding that this was the disease of Rome, the infection of the empire. But did it relieve, or intensify, social tensions? It remains doubtful whether it effectively relieved them.[12]

For the purpose of housing and staging this slaughter, an astonishing new architectural form was devised – the amphitheatre. It could be described as a combination of two theatres, set end to end. This row upon row of consecutive arches, made possible by the use of concrete, has been described as 'the simplicity of genius'. Henry James, on the other hand, called the amphitheatre brutal, monotonous and the reverse of exquisite. However, it was a great architectural achievement, even though it raises questions prompted by the paradoxical emergence of this major, excellent art-form from such deplorable horrors.[13]

Of course the best-known amphitheatre is the Colosseum at Rome, still to be

Figure 16 Reconstruction of the amphitheatre at Nemausus (Nîmes) in Gallia Narbonensis (southern France). Late first century AD or early second.

Paradoxically the deplorable taste for watching gladiators fighting and killing other gladiators, or criminals, or wild animals, produced the great concept of the amphitheatre or arena, made possible by the mastery of concrete and the rows of arches that this mastery could produce. Examples abound: the Colosseum in Rome is the most famous, but there were also superb amphitheatres elsewhere, notably in Gaul, where the arena at Nemausus (Nîmes) rivals that of Arelate (Arles) in grandeur, and exceeds it in modern preservation.

seen today.[14] But it was by no means the only amphitheatre in the Roman world, or even the first. For example, in southern France (Gallia Narbonensis) alone – which was annexed by the Romans at an early date, and virtually became an extension of their Italy – there were six amphitheatres at least, and perhaps as many as eight, some of them quite early.

One of the most remarkable of them is at Nemausus (Nîmes) (Figure 16).[15] This massive ellipse (400 by 300 feet) is in a fair state of repair, and preserves its top storey virtually complete. There were thirty-four rows of seats, able to accommodate some 20,000 spectators. The seats were in three main sections, with 124 exits and 162 sets of stairs. Certainly, the Nemausus amphitheatre was employed for fights with wild beasts. But the low height of the balustrade separating the seats from the arena suggests that it had not been originally intended for that purpose.

Constructed of stone from a quarry at Barutel ($4\frac{1}{2}$ miles to the north of Nîmes) without mortar or clamps, over a concrete core, the amphitheatre has preserved its top storey, in contrast with the amphitheatre at Arelate (Arles), which is, however, similar (although the half-columns flanking its upper arches were Corinthian, not Doric as at Nemausus), and was constructed by the same architect.[16] Unfortunately the dating of the amphitheatre at Nemausus is subject to a good deal of dispute. But it may well have antedated the Roman Colosseum, with which it is compared, though finishing touches could well have been added at Nemausus later on.

> The Roman arena at Nemausus [wrote Henry James] is the rival of those at Verona and Arles; at a respectful distance it emulates the Colosseum. It is a small Colosseum, if I may be allowed the expression, and is in much better preservation than the great circus at Rome. This is especially true of the external walls, with their arches, pillars and cornices. . . . What remains at Nîmes, after all dilapidation is estimated, is astounding. . . . The corridors, the vaults, the staircases, the external casing, are still virtually there.[17]

Nevertheless, although the Nemausus amphitheatre drew on whatever Italian models were available, it improved on them from a technical and visual point of view, by greater emphasis on verticality. The pilasters, or engaged columns, of the façade were carried right up through the entire exterior of the building, with impressive architectural effect.

THE PANHELLENIC STADIUM AT ATHENS

Less bloodthirsty were the horse- and foot-races in stadia, which were more highly favoured sports than the slaughter of men and animals in the eastern part of the empire. Stadia were to be found in cities where games were celebrated, and they were eventually used for other sorts of athletic performance as well. When, in the second century AD, the rich Herodes Atticus constructed and

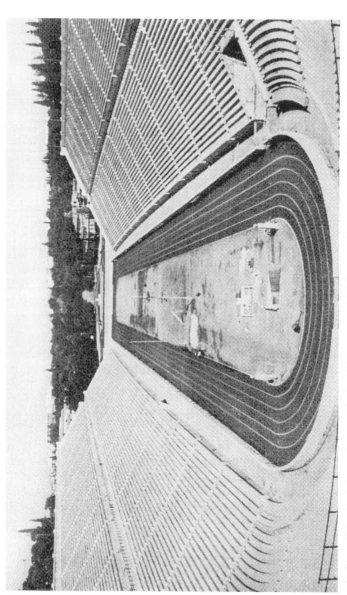

Figure 17 The Stadium of Herodes Atticus at Athens. After its initial construction by Lycurgus (*c.* 390–325/4 BC), rebuilt by Herodes Atticus in AD 135/140–4, during the reign of Hadrian, and again reconstructed in 1896.

A major strength of the largely urbanized Roman empire was the tendency of local aristocracies to honour their home-towns, and perpetuate their own reputations, by expensive building programmes. The wealthy second-century Greek Herodes Atticus, although widely disliked, admired and furthered Hadrian's philhellenism by an enormous programme of construction and reconstruction at his native Athens, as well as at other cities in Greece. One of his principal achievements was the rebuilding of the city's stadium. Such stadia, the scenes of horse and chariot races, were modelled on the Circus Maximus at Rome, although similar races had taken place long before, notably at Olympia in the Peloponnese, and at other centres which had staged the Greek Games.

reconstructed many buildings at Athens, he rebuilt the Panhellenic stadium there, which had first been the work of Lycurgus in 351–326 BC (Figure 17).[18]

This total reconstruction of the stadium was the earliest of Herodes Atticus' lavish presents to his city. The project was so enormous that for the time being it emptied the quarries of Mount Pentelicon of their marble. The stadium, when remodelled, held 50,000 people.

In some ways it echoed the Colosseum at Rome. For example, there was a tunnel at the southern extremity, perhaps (despite what has been said) for wild animals, and a sort of balustrade – more effective than its counterpart in the Nemausus amphitheatre – intended to keep the animals away from the rows of spectators. There were also side-rooms with floors carpeted with mosaics, which probably served as dressing-rooms for the athletes. Within the running-track itself, turnings were marked by herms (marble pillars surmounted by busts). And there was a portico of Doric columns, more than 30 feet high, surmounting the entire structure. The stadium was monumentally approached, from the north, by a bridge across the River Ilissus.

* * *

These different places of entertainment have been deliberately grouped in a single chapter because each of them, in its own way, illustrates one of the themes of this book, a theme that is paradoxical and dual: the enormous influence of the central capital Rome and, conversely, the parts played by regional influences.

Thus the library at Ephesus was a truly imperial undertaking, but served the special needs and architectural requirements and traditions of Ionia. The baths at Aquae Sulis followed a widespread, Rome-centred taste for thermal establishments, and yet placed this within the framework of a local worship and spring. The theatre at Aspendus mirrored the features of a Roman theatre, but was essentially Greek, was created by an architect who if not Greek at least had Greek training, and was designed to respond to the Greek needs of the southern Anatolian coast. The amphitheatre at Nemausus is clearly Roman in inspiration, but catered for a Gallic public: just as the stadium of Herodes Atticus at Athens was a refurbishment of a much older Greek model, catering for Athenian requirements, but in the Roman fashion.

8

ARCHES, BRIDGES, AQUEDUCTS

The Roman ability to use concrete for the making of arches led, as we have seen, to the creation of massive and magnificent amphitheatres consisting of entire arcades, one superimposed upon another. But the same ability led also to the single, independent, free-standing arch, and to the building of bridges and aqueducts.

THE THAMAGUDI ARCH

From the exploitation of the arch as a decoration for some frequented or famous spot it was only a small step for a society as demonstrative and wealthy as that of the Romans to elaborate the same motif in monumental isolation as a 'triumphal arch'. Such arches, incorporating ever more complex ornamental themes and sculptures, became the symbols of empire, and of heroic conquest. To dismiss them as just another unattractive Roman invention is to underrate their artistic value as an eloquent and powerful expression of period mentality, and as one of the empire's unique contributions to architecture.

There were, of course, important triumphal arches at Rome (notably those of Titus and Septimius Severus and Constantine, to mention surviving examples), but for a real proliferation of this type of monument we may turn to other parts of the empire. 'Monument' is the correct term, because these arches did not play any functional part in the external defences of a city, for which, indeed, their openness would have served no purpose. Crowned by bronze statues of emperors or gods, often in horse-drawn chariots – although all this statuary usually vanished a long time ago – the triumphal arches perpetually reminded the local citizenries, throughout the empire, of the power and grandeur of Rome. Frequently they were constructed at the approaches of a town; or they might be erected in one of its public places.[1] Attention has particularly been drawn to North Africa, because monuments of this kind are found there in large numbers and possessing every degree of complexity, from simple archways framed between shallow pilasters up to elaborately adorned, four-way (*quadrifrons*) arches.[2]

Special mention may be accorded to the magnificent triple arch of Thamugadi

(Timgad) (Figure 18), set at a slight angle to the old main street (*decumanus maximus*), of which it had originally been the western town gate.[3] Thamugadi presents one of the clearest pictures of a Roman city in its heyday. Skilfully proportioned, with a strongly controlled overall design, and constructed so as to present a lively contrast between light and darkness, its triple arch, which incorporated a segmental pedimental element framing the niches above its two lateral angles, is known as the 'Arch of Trajan' (AD 98–117), but wrongly. Thamugadi was much favoured by the North African emperor Septimius Severus (193–211), yet the arch slightly antedates his reign, and probably dates from *c.* 165. It belongs to a group of monuments which was thoroughly Roman in origin, but was speedily assuming a distinctively African identity. At Thamugadi there were three other such arches.

THE ALCÁNTARA BRIDGE

If we now turn to bridges, which obviously made use of that same Roman creation the arch, one of the most famous and highest in the Roman world is near Alcántara, over the Tagus (separating Spain from Portugal), 36 miles north-west of Norba (Cáceres) (Figure 19).[4] Constructed of granite, and faced with rusticated ashlar blocks, it spans a river-gorge, by means of six vast semicircular arches – of which the largest is just over 90 feet wide, and 50 feet high at its loftiest point – and carries a road along 630 feet of its length. A triumphal arch erected upon and across this surface of the bridge, marking its central point, carried an inscription, fastened to the arch by two pairs of hands made of bronze. It dated the bridge to Trajan's fifth consulate (AD 103), and named eleven towns of Lusitania (Portugal), which joined together, in a notable feat of co-operation, in order to contribute to the construction of the bridge. On its Spanish side, there was a small shrine housing an altar dedicated by Gaius Julius Lacer, the designer of the bridge, whom the Portuguese honour as their earliest architect whose name is known. The Alcántara bridge, correctly writes S. J. Keay, 'embodies a mastery of concrete as an architectural and engineering medium'.[5]

THE SEGOVIA AQUEDUCT

Just as the arches of bridges spanned water, the arches of aqueducts carried water over land.[6] There were aqueducts throughout the Roman world, and once again there is a magnificent example in Spain. This is the aqueduct at Segovia in central Hispania Tarraconensis (Figure 20).

It is believed that this aqueduct was erected under Augustus, or one of his first successors.[7] Its two-storeyed row of some 120 arches, reaching a maximum height of over 90 feet and crossing the valley for half a mile in the middle of the town, is constructed of large coarse blocks of white granite. The aqueduct extended for 11 miles to the town, from the Rio Frío (near Fuenfría). Its water

Figure 18 'Arch of Trajan' at Thamugadi (Timgad), so-called because it contained a statue of that emperor, dates from somewhat later in the second century AD. Roman mastery of concrete expressed itself in free-standing triumphal arches, designed to celebrate major imperial events. A number still exist at Rome, and are reduplicated in numerous provinces, especially in North Africa, where arches with three passages, or quadrifrontal arches with open sides as well as fronts, are found, all elaborately decorated with sculptures and reliefs. 'Trajan's' at Thamugadi, one of a number of such arches in the town, is a conversion of what was previously a city-gate, and was thus visible to everyone who came up the road from other centres.

Figure 19 The Alcántara Bridge of the second century AD, carrying a Roman road across a river gorge between Norba (Cáceres) and Conimbriga (Coimbra).

The Roman roads were a principal means of controlling the vast territories of the empire. One of the most remarkable Roman bridges still to survive is the Alcántara Bridge across the River Frío, linking the Roman provinces of Baetica (southern Spain) and Lusitania (mainly Portugal). By modern standards, Roman roads may not be classified as works of art. But the finest bridges constructed by their architects are, and were, not only practical but beautiful.

Figure 20 The aqueduct, probably of the first century AD, at Segovia in Spain.
Roman aqueducts brought cherished water long distances from its sources to the baths and the cities. Skilful utilization and development of concrete made it possible to erect the arches of which the aqueducts were formed. An example that can still be seen today is the aqueduct which threads through the town of Segovia in Spain.

flowed through a concrete channel (though concrete and cement are not employed for the remaining parts of the structure).

Outside Segovia, the water passed into a distribution tank, and then it completed its course into the town through another channel. Over the final stretch, in front of the medieval castle (Castillo di Segovia), the ground fell away sharply, so that a much higher row of arches was needed at this point. And this higher row is still to be seen. The planning of the aqueduct was arranged so as to maintain the 1.5 per cent gradient needed to ensure that there was a constant flow of water along its course.

> The Romans could have created a pressure-supply by constructing siphon-conduits. . . . But they did not do so. . . . [Instead they] aimed at using a gravitational flow, aided by small falls in the conduits; Frontinus records a fall of 6 in 100 feet. . . . In spite of some costly failures by local authorities, an expert on the construction of aqueducts, Frontinus, describes these proudly as 'a single testimony to the greatness of the Roman empire. . . . With so many indispensable structures for all these waters you are welcome to compare, if you will, the idle pyramids or all the useless, though famous, works of the Greeks.'[8]

Indeed, as their construction of baths makes clear, the Romans had a respect amounting almost to adoration for running water.[9] It may be true that the Romans did not regard the aqueducts as artistic achievements at all. But that is what they were, all the same.

'The natural countryside', wrote F. E. Brown,

> was dramatically brought to bear on its urban centre by the aqueducts that slanted across it. The great conduits that everywhere fed the thirsty towns, carried by their striding arches, ruled across the accidents of landscape unwavering skylines. So the highways, making straight across the flat, slicing through the rough, or lifted over it on bridges or viaducts, wrought the landscape to man's will. By them it was constricted to a single dimension and a single direction, determined by human uses. By them man was urged forward, kept from straying, and brought to his goal. All this, too, was part of the architecture of the empire, the fixation of space in forms constructed by and for the self-disciplined actions of men.[10]

The aqueducts impressively combine practicality with aesthetic achievement and beauty. Some of them, notably the Segovia aqueduct, still carry water today.

* * *

What an astonishing, empire-wide creation the arches, bridges and aqueducts of the Romans were! The arch, despite its partial and limited Greek antecedents, was a distinctly Roman invention, but it proliferated also, and reached its apogee, in other regions of the Roman world outside Rome. Its prominence in Africa, as a triumphal monument, has been mentioned. And the same provincial ubiquity must be attributed to those other artefacts, the bridge and the aqueduct, which the Romans likewise employed to great effect, not only in Italy, but in far-flung provinces as well: using them to control and dominate the countryside in accordance with their plans and wishes, and creating superb architectural, artistic masterpieces for the purpose.

9

PAGAN BASILICAS

Here the Romans come very easily into the centre of the picture, because the basilica was their invention (even though it harked back, in some respects – as its name suggests – to the Greek peristyle and colonnaded piazza). The Roman basilica was essentially a large building used for official purposes. In strict architectural usage, say Boethius and Ward-Perkins, it was

> an elongated rectangular building with an internal ambulatory enclosing a taller central area, or else with a central nave and lateral aisles, in either case lit by a clerestory: often provided with one or more apses or tribunes. Originally a roofed extension of the Forum for the use of the public, from the Late Republic onwards it was used for a variety of official purposes, notably judicial. During the Empire the term came to be used of any hall that was basilican in plan, irrespective of its purpose; and also of any large covered hall, irrespective of its plan.[1]

Basilicas in Rome go back to the republic, and their remains of that date in the city are well worth inspection. But perhaps the most imposing of all today are imperial examples, represented, for instance, by the Severan Basilica at Lepcis Magna (Lebda) in Libya (Figure 21), the birthplace of the Emperor Septimius Severus (193–211), who enriched his home town with this and many other buildings. His basilica at Lepcis Magna was a vast colonnaded hall, with a central, ornamented apse at each extremity.[2] It was 62 feet wide, and there were galleries above the side-aisles, giving a total height estimated at over 100 feet. Along the north-eastern façade ran an enclosed street. The façade itself was ornate and individual. Pedestals were lavishly employed to provide additional height for this basilica. In general, height, as well as grace, was stressed, and there was ample employment of first-class masonry, supplemented by the variegated use of brightly coloured marbles and elaborate, deeply incised, architectural ornamentation. Rings of acanthus foliage appeared between bases and columns.

It must be concluded that the basilica at Lepcis Magna, and the other buildings of Severan date at the city were probably designed by one single architect. It has been conjectured that he was a newcomer to North Africa.

Figure 21 The Severan Basilica (of Septimius Severus) at Lepcis Magna (Lebda) in Libya (AD 216).

The basilica was essentially a Roman invention, found in late republican Rome: an all-purpose hall, longitudinal in shape, usually with two aisles separated from the higher nave by rows of columns, and with a flat roof. It terminated in an apse, beneath which usually stood a statue.

During the Roman imperial period basilicas were reduplicated all over the empire, usually close to the main *fora* of cities. An example can still be seen, or traced, at Lepcis Magna. Although originating at an earlier date, it benefited from the munificence of Septimius Severus, who came from Lepcis Magna, and bears witness to the rise of the provinces towards competition or equality with Rome.

Indeed, it seems highly probable that both he and many of his assistants (who left their signatures on various parts of the basilica) originated from the Greek-speaking world, and probably from Asia Minor. In particular, the suggestion has been made that these skilled craftsmen came from the island of Proconnesus (Marmara) in the Propontis (Sea of Marmara). Attic, Egyptian and Syrian details can be detected;[3] but also a western, Roman spirit. The author's commission must have been to follow Roman models. But the architectural vocabulary, materials and methods that he used in carrying out his commission were those of his own background and training.

THE BASILICA OF MAXENTIUS

By the fourth century, the pagan basilica had become an audience-hall for emperors, and two examples of this phenomenon have partially survived, the Basilica of Maxentius (Constantine) in Rome, beside the Forum, and the contemporary basilica at Augusta Trevirorum (Trier) on the River Mosella (Moselle), in Gallia Belgica.

As regards the former of these edifices – and here we have briefly to leave the provinces for their Roman source of inspiration itself – it is the most magnificent building in the whole Forum, standing a little more than 100 yards east of the Basilica Aemilia, upon the Sacred Way. It is the 'New' Basilica, begun by Maxentius (306–12) – the last pagan emperor to choose Rome for his capital – and completed by his victor Constantine the Great (312–37) (Figure 22).

This edifice was a rectangle terminating at its north-west and north-east ends in apses, of which the latter survives. It is 350 feet long (north-west/south-east) and nearly 200 feet in width (north-east/south-west). It is sometimes fashionable to decry mere size, but when the scale is as vast as this, and when, as here, it is achieved by architecture of outstanding brilliance, such dimensions add a new and fresh character to a building. As Sir Mortimer Wheeler remarks, the crowning gift of the Roman empire to architecture was magnitude.[4] With magnitude, of course, went many other qualities, but most of them were in some measure attendant upon magnitude; they were literally of epoch-making importance.

The Basilica of Maxentius was divided, on both its short and its long axis, into a nave and two aisles; that is to say, the long nave and aisles were criss-crossed by shorter ones. The divisions between the naves and their aisles consisted of four huge piers – only four, compared with the seventy-four columns of the Basilica Julia which had been only one-third as large. Just in front of the piers stood Corinthian columns 47 feet high, made of a creamy, red-veined marble from the Propontis (Sea of Marmara). They have vanished from the site, but one, converted to a Christian purpose, can still be seen in another part of Rome, the Piazza Santa Maria Maggiore. The columns of the Basilica of Maxentius, however, did not bear the weight of the huge vaults, which were directly carried by the concrete-cored piers beside which the columns were little more than decorative attachments.

Figure 22   The Basilica of Maxentius at Rome, later known as the Basilica of Constantine (AD 306–37), who reorientated the building.
A new departure, the basilica's roof was not flat but vaulted. And this vaulting and the three huge surviving arches bear witness to the immensity of the Roman innovations, based on concrete, which made such buildings possible. A grandiose demonstration of the Roman supremacy which Constantine claimed to embody, this was the last great architectural masterpiece erected in pagan Rome.

And so, in spite of earthquakes and other devastations, a large part of this building, the three terminal spans (north-east) of the shorter nave and aisles, continued to stand even after their columns had gone. And they still stand today: three arches of the same size, 80 feet high and 67 feet across, the width of the present St Peter's (whose architects studied the building carefully). The original tunnel-vaulting, too, can still be seen, with its sunken ornamental panels. The walls flanking the aisles are broken by two rows of great, arched windows. The surviving, shorter nave, on the other hand, terminates in a rounded apse, which likewise survives. It develops, on an enormous scale, the apsidal construction which had long been a feature of Roman architecture.

When Maxentius started the Basilica, this apse on the shorter axis did not exist, for, according to his version, the only apse was on the longer axis, as its north-western extremity facing the Forum, and the only entrance consisted of a portico at the opposite end. The long nave which extended between this entrance and apse has not survived, but unlike the shorter nave it was taller than its aisles, rising to a height of no less than 115 feet, higher than Westminster Abbey. Constantine, however, altered this plan in *c.* AD 313, making the shorter axis the main one instead. With this in mind he constructed a further portico on the SW side upon the Sacred Way. It was framed by porphyry columns, which partly survive, and was approached by a long flight of steps. Inside, at the far end, rose a new apse, which is the one we see today. It was set apart by a lofty columned balustrade, and apparently served to house the tribunal which, according to the tradition for Basilicas, heard legal cases in the building.

The walls were punctuated with niches. What remains today is brick-faced; originally there were marble facings up to a certain height, and above came a covering of stucco. The white stucco on the vaults was overlaid by gilding and paint, and there was sculptural decoration too, for part of a frieze of sea-gods and nymphs is preserved in the Forum Museum. The pavement was made of variegated marbles, red, green, yellow and white.

Hitherto the elevated naves of Basilicas had possessed windowed walls extending beside and above the roofs of their lateral aisles; and sometimes, though not here in the Roman Forum, they had terminated in apses. The longer nave of the Basilica of Maxentius repeated both these features, but they were transformed not only in scale but in the manner of their application. For one thing, the roof was not flat but vaulted . . . [like] the enormous arched, side-chapelled throne room that the Persians had erected late in the previous century at their capital Ctesiphon on the Tigris.

And yet the basic concept of the Basilica of Maxentius was Roman, for it was founded on Roman models . . . above all on the huge central halls that formed the divisions of Roman Baths. What had been done here was to plan a structure of the same kind but to design it in detached isolation as a separate building. . . .

Such were the models for the New Basilica. . . . [Its] huge rounded windows, such as can still be seen at the ends of the shorter aisles . . . not only introduced a novel method of lighting but created an emphatic rhythmical relation of window to wall. The walls look medieval, and the shape of the windows anticipates Romanesque. . . . The new building, then, is a prototype of the cathedrals of the future. And it foreshadows their vaulted naves as well. . . . Moreover, as in certain earlier buildings, another big anti-classical step had also been taken. The columns attached to the arches were no longer surmounted by continuous horizontal blocks, those entablatures which throughout the classical age had been an obligatory accompaniment of the columnar form. . . . The shorter naves and aisles show arches which exist quite independently of the columns that stood decoratively in front of their piers.

But the columns served a second purpose as well, for from above their lintels soared even higher arches, now vanished, which rose to the heights of the ceiling vaults of the longer, higher nave and formed an angle with them.

All this, then, seems anticipatory of the Middle Ages. Nevertheless . . . it was not until seven hundred more years had passed that the architects of cathedrals began to use vaults competing in size and boldness with this masterpiece of the early fourth century AD.[5]

As one walks around and observes the immense Basilica of Maxentius – although ancient literary soruces are almost silent on the subject – one is inspired by its lofty spaciousness, which conveys a very different impression from the spatial limits imposed by the horizontal and vertical dimensions of the temples that stood nearby in the Roman Forum. Any visitor is 'strangely subdued by a feeling of his [or her] own small insignificance and . . . the greater unity into which he [or she] has entered and of which he [or she] now becomes more thoroughly a part'.[6]

For this was one of the architectural marvels of the Roman world. Breaking with classical tradition, its plan eclipses all earlier basilicas in grandeur and brilliance. The interior must have seemed to soar upwards without weight: for every wall-space was excavated into windows or niches; the coffering of the ceiling was made to look like trellis open to the sky; and the octagons and lozenges at the pavement reinforce this illusion, by seeming like a reflection of that coffering. Moreover, there was a novel, creative relationship between wall and window. And there was a new, conscious rhythm in the continuous series of arches.[7]

THE BASILICA OF AUGUSTA TREVIRORUM

Another, very different, late Roman basilica was at Augusta Trevirorum (Trier)

Figure 23 The Aula Palatina at Augusta Trevirorum (Trier) on the River Mosella (Moselle), sometimes known as the city's basilica, was erected in the time of Constantine I the Great (AD 306–37), on the site of an older apsed hall.
This building, which still stands today, has experienced various adaptations, but the main lines of the original structure are still to be seen. Although its design owes something to the basilican formula, it was primarily an audience hall in which the ruler held court. The building's shape and large rounded windows bear witness to its date and to the architectural forms and tastes of the time, when Augusta Trevirorum was an imperial headquarters and one of the principal cities of the empire.

on the River Mosella (Moselle) (Figure 23).

The Basilica of Augusta Trevirorum, which had been the capital of Constantine's father Constantius I Chlorus, who had started systematic building projects there, is of particular interest because the main lines of its construction by Constantine can, unusually, still be seen. It was the Audience Hall, the *Aula Palatina*, of his palace there (and has been a Lutheran church since 1856). The building was begun in *c.* 306, and was praised by a panegyrist in 310.

More than 2,400 metres square, with no aisles but an apse, its walls pierced with pipes to provide heating, and equipped with a space under the floor to secure the luxurious circulation of hot air, the walls of the Basilica are constructed of brick, which was originally, in the interior, concealed behind marble slabs and a plaster covering, and this covering was painted, around its two tiers of windows, with Cupids and ochre-tinted tendrils of vines, against a red background. Above the windows, too, the plaster was decorated with painting, and the arches which crowned the windows were adorned with mosaics, while geometric designs of multicoloured marble and gilt glass covered the lower part of the walls.

The building was very lofty, with its vault one hundred feet above the ground, and was no less than 250 feet long. Its pavement displayed a honeycomb pattern in black and white, and a similar design was to be seen in the narthex. In the middle of the apse was a platform, on which stood the emperor's throne. It was here that he sat for ceremonial celebrations, designed to announce victories or new laws, or to receive envoys from foreign lands. The eyes of his audience lifted into this massive, ornate space, rich in every tint of gold and red and green and yellow, and moved onto the climactic point of the imperial throne within the apse. Planned so as to show off the platform on which Constantine sat, this apse was resplendent with mosaics, under a coffered and gilded ceiling.[8]

This achievement was due to the Roman use of cheap, strong, malleable, lightweight, thrustless concrete, of which mention has already been made; already developing in the second century BC, it had freed architects from the static necessities of masonry. The exploitation of this material had led to the arcades of amphitheatres and the free-standing triumphal arches in which the empire abounded. But it also led to the huge barrel-vaults of baths, and the massive cross-vaults in the basilicas – buildings undreamt of by the Greeks, but now created with the utmost sophistication and skill.

*　　*　　*

The basilica, whatever its partial origins elsewhere, was, it should be repeated, an essentially Roman invention, although it lent itself to manifold adaptations in conformity with the special requirements of the provinces. And it lent itself, also, to changes – amounting to total transformation – even at Rome itself. As we shall see in the next chapter, it also made an immense contribution to the development of church-building, once the empire had become Christian.

CHRISTIAN ARCHITECTURE

There has been a lot of argument about the slowness and tact of Constantine I the Great (AD 306–37) in displaying his Christianity, especially at Rome itself where the ruling class (not to speak of the army) was predominantly pagan. Tactful he was, yet he displayed his new allegiance unmistakably by the creation of new Christian churches, unparalleled by any comparable contemporary developments in regard to the temples of paganism.

In particular, Constantine adapted the old pagan basilica – which has been discussed in Chapter 9 – so as to make it the model of his great Christian churches. These Christian basilicas were once again, very often, rectangular, longitudinal edifices. Entry was from a spacious courtyard, and the interior consisted of a nave with side-aisles separated from it by arched rows of columns. Above these columns stood brick walls standing directly upon the arches (since the aisles were lower than the nave), and generally containing windows. There was a large arch, too, separating this congregational part of the Christian basilica from the apse, which framed an altar surmounted by a canopy (*baldacchino*) and contains the throne (*cathedra*) of the bishop.

> The roofs of these Christian Basilicas did not normally consist of cross-vaulting. Instead they were flat and made of wood, which was either visible or concealed by a ceiling. The great vaults of earlier Roman secular buildings (including the Basilica of Maxentius, though not other pagan Basilicas) seemed too worldly and redolent of unchristian times. Besides, they would have impeded the axial flow of naves and aisles which was planned to attract the gaze of Christian worshippers towards the apse and its altar.
>
> Nevertheless, these splendid churches, which set such a stamp on the future, owed a great many other features to the pagan Basilicas of the past, which had served at one and the same time as market, meeting-place and law court (with a tribunal where the imperial and then episcopal thrones were placed later). Indeed, these new Christian buildings owed these pagan Basilicas the main lines of their entire structure, including the arrangement of the windows. And yet the whole ineluctable tide of the

churches' direction, leading so potently towards the apse and the altar, was not the same as the more passive and relaxed, circumambient and counter-flowing, orientation of the pagan basilicas of the past.[1]

As regards other precedents, the Christian basilica, with its internal rows of columns, has been defined as a Greek temple turned inside out. A more immediate and recent model, however, was supplied by the halls of audience in the palaces of cities such as Augusta Trevirorum (Trier) and Spalatum (Split). The manner in which the complicated ceremonial of the halls of audience at those palaces was taken over by the Christian liturgy is mirrored and echoed in the architecture of the new Christian churches. The altar beneath the canopy of such churches resembled the throne of an emperor in his *palatium sacrum*, and the triumphal chancel-arch was derived from the gable of imperial glorification in the pagan halls.

With these prototypes to look back upon and, to some extent, to copy,

> The interiors of the churches as a whole were spacious, dignified and designed to encourage spiritual elevation. . . . The turning of worshippers' eyes towards the apse and the altar was encouraged and heightened by everything . . . 'the measured pace of columns, the trajectory of horizon-tals, the side-lighted tunnel of space, the enframing arch, the terminal apse'. . . . The essence of the whole dramatic arrangement was light. . . . In all Christian churches, throughout the empire, while there is holy dusk below, there is light, incorporeal and insubstantial, above. And in every Christian church, too, this light of the sun was 'enhanced by brilliant internal colouring, provided by paintings and mosaics and precious metal objects and jewelled robes, of which oil wicks and candles prolonged the shimmerings and glintings into the night'. Colour and light more than anything else brought animation to this Christian architecture, and it was helped onwards by numerous donations, many of which came from the emperor himself. Lists of the imperial gifts to churches abound with jewelled altarcloths, and chalices, patens, jugs and jars, and gold and silver chandeliers and candlesticks and lamps.[2]

These were scenes of sparkling brilliance. Later in the century priests protested about the excessive luxury involved in the creation of such splendour. For, indeed, the construction and maintenance of these churches required enormous endowments, and the expenditure of a great deal of money, much of which had to be found from the already oppressive taxation that Constantine imposed upon the empire.

> However, there is an irritating and disappointing feature in any study of Constantinian ecclesiastical architecture. It resides in the fact that nearly all Constantine's churches have totally, or almost totally, disappeared – vanished off the face of the earth. This is partly because, although they

represented such a major achievement, and were replete with expensive objects and materials, they were often poorly constructed, because there were not enough good architects and builders to cope with this immense programme.[3] But another reason for their disappearance is that in many cases they and their sites were so greatly revered that later emperors, for their own glory, replaced them with their own new constructions.

Nevertheless, by recourse to literary descriptions and archaeology, we can get quite a good idea of what Constantine's massive and extravagant ecclesiastical building programme amounted to – of what, that is to say, most of his churches were like.[4]

Constantine's most astonishing building was St Peter's (Figure 24), decided upon in 324–6, and constructed from *c.* 335, although, as so often, it has been thoroughly replaced by later churches on the same site: so that we have to rely on old descriptions and paintings and on archaeological researches to obtain some idea of how the original building appeared. As a prime part of Constantine's attempt to give a Christian stamp to Rome, it was designed to house numerous pilgrims, coming to venerate the place where St Peter was believed to have met his death and to have been buried.

Although so little of Constantinian pre-Renaissance St Peter's is now extant, some additional idea of what the basilicas of Constantine looked like can be obtained from the cathedral at Aquileia, in north-eastern Italy. Replacing a house-church, this cathedral was finished before AD 319 and perhaps as early as 313. Two principal, parallel halls, one extending to the east and the other to the west, were linked at their extremities by a transverse chamber, off which lay a square room, serving as a baptistery.

The design has been revealed by excavations. Although there is an eleventh-century cathedral on top of the ancient structures, the Constantinian walls of the south hall still survive to a considerable extent, embedded in the medieval walls. Each of the two principal ancient halls measured about 66 by 122 feet, and each was divided into a nave and two aisles (of the same width as the nave). The naves contained six piers of columns, supporting ceilings that were flat. There was also at least one transverse, coffered barrel-vault, in the east bay of the southern hall. It was made of cane.

So this was a 'double cathedral', a formula of distinctly regional character, since a large number of Constantinian and slightly later churches in the Adriatic region were laid out in a similar dual fashion.

BASILICA OF S. MARIA MAGGIORE, ROME

Informative, too, is the Basilica of S. Maria Maggiore at Rome (Figure 25)[5] – to which we have to turn once again for vital evidence. Although this church has been extensively altered and adapted, its interior is still of unique historical value, because it is the only example of a great Roman basilica that has, in its

CONTIGNATIO·TE CTI·PARTIS
VETER·BASILSVB·PAVLO·V·
DEMOLITAE·

Figure 24 Painting showing the original appearance of the Constantinian Basilica of St Peter at Rome, subsequently obliterated and reconstructed during the Renaissance.

In establishing Christianity as the state religion, Constantine I the Great created two huge churches in Rome itself: the Basilica of St John Lateran, and the Basilica of St Peter.

The latter was erected at huge cost over a pagan necropolis, thought to have been the burial-place of St Peter; a chunk had to be cut out of the Vatican hill. Unfortunately, most of the original building has disappeared. But it is clear from paintings and excavations how the basilican tradition was adapted to the new Christian requirements (hitherto humbly met by house-churches).

Figure 25 Interior of the Basilica of Santa Maria Maggiore at Rome. True, the side-chapels and ceilings were introduced subsequently, and other alterations have taken place. But the naves and aisles, the two colonnades that separate them, and the mosaic-covered apse, are still reminiscent of late antiquity and its basilicas. The two principal exteriors of the church echo epochs much nearer to our own and give little idea of this late imperial grandeur.

main lines, been preserved, and has thus retained its original character.[6] The interior of this building (279 feet long and 60 wide) is divided into a broad nave and two lateral aisles by thirty-six antique Ionic columns of brightly coloured marble from Mount Hymettus in Greece, supplemented by four columns of granite. These colonnades support a continuous entablature, and a row of fluted Corinthian pilasters, erected above the columns separating the nave from the aisles. Along the entablature stand thirty-six mosaic panels offering scenes from the New Testament. All but a few of those near the door (which are modern replicas) date from the time of Pope Sixtus III, who enlarged the church to its present dimensions in AD 432, during the reign of the western emperor Valentinian III (425–55). As Richard Krautheimer emphasizes,

> a 'classical revival' comes decisively to the fore under Pope Sixtus III (432–40). . . . The Basilica of S. Maria Maggiore best represents the 'Sixtine Renaissance'. . . . The long rows of classical columns with Ionic capitals carry a 'classical' entabulature and lead the way to the Triumphal Arch which continued into the original apse vault. On the nave walls monumental pilasters formed an upper order . . . carrying a stucco frieze of the purest classical design. . . . Overall design and details breathe a spirit more retrospective than the live classicism of Constantinople.[7]

BASILICA OF ST JOHN STUDIOS, CONSTANTINOPLE

There in Constantinople, St John Studios, founded in 463 by the patriarch Studios, is the oldest existing, unaltered church of the basilican type (Figure 26). Unaltered, that is to say, but in ruins, as far as the church itself is concerned – of the monastery of St John the Baptist, to which it was attached, nothing remains. Yet, ruined though the basilica is (largely because of fires in 1782 and 1920, and an earthquake in 1894), its principal features can be reconstructed and turn out to be not entirely different from those of S. Maria Maggiore at Rome.

Almost square in shape, the church of St John Studios had a short nave, surmounted by galleries on three sides. And this nave was separated from the aisles by rows of columns made of green marble, surmounted by an entablature on which stood shorter, greyish, veined columns with graceful Ionic capitals. This entablature carried an acanthus frieze. The walls of the basilica were covered, inside, with marble plaques; and it is supposed that, up above, the walls of the galleries were painted. The vault in the apse was adorned with a mosaic, and above the apse are five small arched windows.

The masonry of the church is concrete, faced with mortared brick, which is sometimes diversified by the employment of stone. The façade of the basilica was preceded by a porch (narthex), flanked by a colonnade containing another acanthus frieze and displaying Corinthian capitals. The narthex was reached from the interior of the church by three doors, one leading from the central nave and the others from the two aisles.

Figure 26 The Basilica of St John Studios at Constantinople (the former Byzantium).

A more or less unspoilt and unaltered example of the Constantinian Christian basilica, the remains of the longitudinal church give an idea of the Christian places of worship which Constantine the Great caused to be erected all over the empire. True, they are not very complete, but they are better than nothing — and rare, because Constantinian structures, at Constantinople, as elsewhere, were so frequently built over by later edifices (for example, Santa Sophia in the same city).

Everything speaks [writes Krautheimer] of the preservation and strength of a classical tradition nurtured by Constantinian and post-Constantinian sources. . . . However, the decoration is filled with a new life, created largely by the contrasts of dark background and raised design of light and shade.[8]

The ruins of the church [adds M. Pereira], open to the sky, are folded in tranquillity. It is a place of silence. Its epitome is peace.

And he particularly admired six columns of *verde antico*, 'pale and cold and green'.[9]

EVIDENCE OF EARLY CHRISTIAN BASILICAS

It is a commonplace that Rome created Christianity, but the debt of early Christian architecture to the architecture of the Roman empire deserves more exact definition. In the first place, the early Christian basilica was created, for the most part, out of the pagan Roman basilica. True, the early Christian basilica is rather hard to find, because, as we saw, Contantinian and subsequent Christian buildings became so famous that they were abundantly altered and transformed. But this type of building was also transported to the provinces, where its principal features can sometimes be reconstructed, as has been noted.

MEMORIAE AND *MARTYRIA*

The early Christians were also concerned to erect *memoriae* or *martyria*, in honour of their saints, either as extensions and end-pieces of longitudinal basilicas or independently, on their own, as free-standing buildings. These last were centralized structures, which were not an altogether novel idea (witness the Pantheon at Rome, and the Mausoleum of Diocletian at Spalatum [Split][Figure 27], and of Galerius at Thessalonica [Salonica]). But it was the Christians who developed these centralized buildings much more widely, in various regions which did not cease, however, at the same time, to maintain traditions of their own. This, in other words, was another formula which the provinces inherited from the architecture of the pagan Roman empire and developed in their own fashion, or rather in a number of different fashions, in accordance with the characters and peculiarities of the various regions in which they erected churches.

In these centralized Christian structures – which were usually rotundas, or domed polyhedrons – the worshippers were massed together in a pool of space, with darkness all round this luminous core. They stood, as it were, in a central well of transcendent light, hedged in by the shadows that surrounded them, and magnetized by the altar or monument that stood in their midst.

At S. Maria Maggiore in Rome and St John Studios at Constantinople we

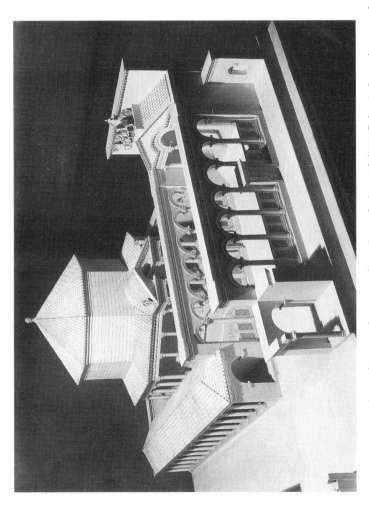

Figure 27 The mausoleum of the Emperor Diocletian (d. AD 313) forms part of his palace at Spalatum (Split) in Dalmatia. It stood on an 11-foot podium within a peristyle of Corinthian columns. The massive walls were reduced internally by deep niches alternately round and rectangular. Between the niches, Corinthian columns carried an engaged entablature, and were surmounted by smaller columns. Externally, the building is octagonal, and the dome an octagonal pyramid, though internally circular.

Such centralized structures were not new. But they were the immediate forerunners of the centralized *martyria* and *memoriae* which were either attached to the east ends of longitudinal Christian basilicas, or stood separately from them, as did Christian baptisteries as well.

have seen simple basilicas, without a centralized *memoria* or *martyrium* at the far end. But at St Peter's such a combined structure existed, because, after all, the shrine of the saint, the *memoria*, had become the main purpose of the longitudinal basilica to which it was now attached.

In order to create the shrine, way back in the second century AD, since this was a pagan necropolis, a number of pagan tomb chambers had had to be filled in, and their upper portions obliterated. When Constantine built his basilica and a new *memoria* or *martyrium*, he only left the top part of the old second-century *memoria* of St Peter, near the western extremity of the site.

The difficulties and expenses he incurred in surmounting the obstacles which the location presented are sufficient proof in themselves, if no other evidence existed, that the building was created to house the *memoria* of the venerated apostle.

> [Owing to] the dual nature of the building that came to be erected . . . the nave and aisles did not simply terminate in a chancel, according to the more normal basilica pattern. Instead they were prolonged by an enormous transverse structure, a sort of transept, towards which the eyes and steps of the worshippers were led. It was this transverse structure which enshrined the earlier monument of St Peter, and was therefore the focal point of the entire building. Surrounded by a bronze balustrade, the monument was also surmounted by a splendid canopy (*baldacchino*), resting on four spiral columns bearing reliefs of vine scrolls.
>
> This was, therefore, a church combined with a very special *martyrium*, the shrine of the martyred Peter himself, and it was destined in consequence to retain its exceptional fame and sanctity throughout subsequent generations. . . . However, this edifice took a long time to build, and by the time of Constantine's death in 337 only the portions that stood above the monument to Peter had been completed.[10]

> These *martyria*, centralized buildings devoted to the memory and cult of a Christian martyr, came into being in response to a marked development in religious feeling.
>
> Burials [in Roman paganism] were forbidden within the city walls. . . . [But] that prohibition was gradually bypassed. In particular, the cult of martyrs promulgated by the early Church spread the belief that martyrs were not dead, but were presently alive, their bones and relics emanating power in the form of miraculous acts and visions. No longer the bones of the dead, they were translated from cemeteries into places of honour within churches which lay inside the city walls.[11]

The existence of a *martyrium* or *memoria*, towards the end of a longitudinal basilica, is paralleled in a number of cities besides Rome.[12] The space available for such shrines was not large enough to hold the vast numbers of people who wished to attend the memorial celebrations and commemorative banquets that took place there.[13] Equally, there was not space for the numerous people whose desire it was that they should be buried near the martyr's body, aspiring after that proximity as an assurance that they themselves would, in their afterlife, be saved. The funeral banquets had grown to a monstrous size, and the crowds got out of hand: there was drunkenness and over-eating and improper dancing, and dirty songs and fighting. Longitudinal basilicas were clearly unable to cope with these disorderly mobs. And that is partly why special *martyria* or *memoriae* were erected over the tomb of the martyr and as part, or at the end, of the basilica, in order to concentrate, there, on the commemorative functions that were now required. One *martyrium*, upon the graveyard of the Five Martyrs at Kapljuč (near Salonae; *c.* AD 350), displays one variety of this process of adaptation. For while one half of the edifice assumed the outline of a longitudinal basilica, the other half became a covered graveyard for the faithful, a *memoria* dedicated to the Five Martyrs.

MEMORIA AT THE CHURCH OF THE HOLY SEPULCHRE, JERUSALEM

At Jerusalem, too, a centralized *memoria* arose at the far end of the Church of the Anastasis (Resurrection), i.e. of the Holy Sepulchre; the *memoria* enclosed what was believed to be the Sepulchre of Christ (Figure 28).[14] The church, which was approached through a semicircular colonnaded porch, appears to have been in use, with its *memoria*, perhaps as early as 350 – thirteen years after Constantine's death – or, at the latest, by 380.

Although this *memoria* has often been altered and remodelled, we can form an approximate idea of its original plan. It was a massive, domed rotunda, measuring 55 feet across, its principal chamber surrounded by an ambulatory. The central point and *raison d'être* of the edifice lay in the middle. For this was thought to be the site of Christ's Sepulchre, and a canopy was erected over the holy spot. In case too many faithful flocked in, so that there would not be adequate room for them on the ground floor, a gallery was constructed above the ambulatory of the *memoria* for their accommodation.

Not much remains of the original fourth-century building at Jerusalem today – only sparse, though carefully noted, fragments of the lower level of the ambulatory wall. But we know enough about this early church to see that it followed a strong, antique, pagan tradition: the tradition of imperial *mausolea* and *heroa*. And now the tradition gained new life.

The Constantinian church has been thoroughly examined by S. Gibson and J. E. Taylor, in *Beneath the Church of the Holy Sepulchre, Jerusalem* (1994):[15]

Soon after Constantine defeated his rival Licinius in 324 and became emperor of the East as well as the West, he ordered that the Hadrianic

Figure 28 The *rotunda* (round structure) at the far end of the Church of the Anastasis (Resurrection) – generally known as the Holy Sepulchre – at Jerusalem. Reconstruction derived from an engraving by J. Callot, showing how it looked in 1609.

This outstanding *memoria*, the centralized east end of the basilica, was believed to stand on the very spot where Jesus Christ was crucified. Today one has to look carefully at the walls in order to locate even traces of the original centralized building, but records and excavations have made it possible to form some idea of what it was like.

temple of Venus in Jerusalem [second century AD] should be torn down and that a new Christian basilica be built on the site. The literary starting point for a discussion of the Contantinian structures has always been Eusebius's description in his *Life of Constantine.* . . . The work echoes the style of a panegyric. . . . He is not particularly concerned with recording the architectural details of the basilica and, to the dismay of scholars, seems never to have written the detailed description he promised.

[Two walls] belong to the foundations of Constantine's basilica, which was dedicated in September, 335. . . . [One], the eastern continuation of the northern wall of the Chapel of St Helena . . . was built of large stones 46–65 cm. deep, encasing a core of mortar and rubble. The joints between the stones were coated with hard grey mortar. Small stones and earth can still be seen adhering to the surface of this mortar, suggesting that the entire area was filled in very soon after the construction of the wall had been completed, while the mortar was still wet. . . . The smooth-faced stones may have been taken from dismantled Hadrianic superstructures. . . . [The other Constantinian wall] is located on the eastern side of the excavations. . . . It consists of eleven courses of stones . . . with a coating of grey mortar in the joints between the stones. . . .

The general layout of the Constantinian basilica, the Martyrium, is reasonably certain. At the time when the basilica was dedicated, in AD 335, the Anastasis clearly had not yet been built. . . . [It] was not part of Constantine's plan. The Anastasis was most likely constructed during the latter part of the reign of Constantius II (AD 337–61), who consolidated the programme of Christianisation and church building begun by his father Constantine. . . .

Many scholars have doubted whether the wood alleged to be from Christ's cross was really found in the time of Constantine. Drake's recent re-examination of the legend has now proved that these doubts are unjustified. . . . Eusebius says that wood was around the building site, and there is a chance that a piece of the wood was heralded as deriving from the cross, a belief which Eusebius held in scant regard. However, it would not have been wise for Eusebius to have been publicly sceptical. It would appear that the emperor Constantine himself believed that wood from the cross was found at the site. The basilica was constructed, not to honour the tomb, but to honour the 'saving sign' of the cross. As Drake has recently suggested, it seems very likely that the dome, described by Eusebius as the main part of the basilica, was designed to enshrine the place, somewhere beneath the apse or altar, where the wood of the cross was discovered. . . . The finding of the wood of the cross caused a sensation.

And so this church became the most venerated site in Christendom, and the most powerful focus of pilgrim attraction.

*   *   *

But let us consider, finally, the aims of Constantine, who inspired its construction, and the possibilities open to him. He was accustomed to insist on monumental public structures, adorned with a great quantity of precious objects. And, as we said earlier, he placed churches at the very summit of public monumental architecture, employing modified versions of classical, pagan traditions in their design. However, he also had to bear in mind local requirements and resources, which were duly set out in writing by the bishop of the region, just as the provincial governor or his delegate set out those of secular buildings. Moreover, it was necessary to consider what materials were locally available and procurable (if what was needed could not be got locally, it might be necessary to obtain materials from abroad). It was also advisable to examine closely the background of the architect – once again, he might be a local man, or he might have to be brought in from abroad – and to find out how well informed he was about the type of building that was required, and whether he was acquainted with the specimens of that sort of construction which had already been erected elsewhere.

Part III

OTHER ARTS

PAINTINGS, STUCCO, TEXTILES

WALL-PAINTINGS

There was a good deal of Roman painting – which then, as now, made a more direct appeal than either architecture or portraiture to the taste of the public – much of it (again as now) mediocre, but a certain amount first-class.[1] We know a good deal about these pictures, but from an unbalanced, limited point of view, because of the survival of so much of Pompeii and Herculaneum and Stabiae, and of some of the mummy-paintings from Egypt, but of not much else besides.

At Pompeii and Herculaneum and Stabiae we see

> the evolution of an art form of paramount importance in the ancient world: the interior decoration of the Roman villa. These paintings provide a vivid reflection of daily life in ancient times; through them, we gain insight into the aesthetic experience of Rome and are able to see which themes were considered important in Roman society. . . . We must bear in mind that these paintings were not created in isolation. They were part of a life-style, important expressions of Roman culture and a reflection of the values of the period. Today, they provide an incomparable source of information concerning that culture, the tastes and concerns of its people, and the subjects that most interested the Roman world. In these paintings, antiquity comes to life.[2]

The mural paintings in the cities of Vesuvius and elsewhere in the Roman empire (that is to say, those pictures that were not destined for easels) were put straight on to the walls of the rooms in the houses.

> Wall-paintings . . . constitute, all in all, the most remarkable aspect of Pompeii and Herculaneum. . . . No Roman equivalents on anything like a comparable scale, and absolutely no Greek wall-paintings at all, have come down to us through the centuries. For painting, except in the less important medium of ceramics, is the most fragile of art-forms, and the most unlikely to survive except in very special conditions. And so the

deaths of the two cities, as Goethe remarked, were significant not so much for the transitoriness of life as for the perpetuity of art. . . . [These paintings] seldom fail to be light, airy, gay and graceful, seeking to charm and succeeding in doing so, and suggesting a general, widespread high standard of visual civilization, which extended quite a way down the social scale, has never been exceeded in any subsequent age, and is very markedly superior to what could be found in any town of comparable size today. . . .

Yet the art of this region was not entirely, or even principally, a serious art. It is true that a painter of the time was working for clients who were remarkably alive to the higher points of harmony and good taste, especially in aesthetic matters. But what these patrons really wanted was just to enjoy the walls of their houses; and they were able to appreciate a sophisticated and mildly malicious light-heartedness. . . .

The first step in creating these pictures was to apply to the wall two or three carefully treated layers of limestone plaster, mixed with calcite and sand. Then the background of the picture was painted in, and left to dry. When it was dry, the figures and ornaments were added. The colours were mixed with soapy limestone, and some kind of glue and wax was added to create a shiny surface. By these means the paintings acquired great durability and brilliance. The pigments employed in antiquity were chiefly earth colours such as ochres, mineral colours such as carbonate of copper, and dyes of vegetables and animal origin.

The technique was by no means an easy one to master, and required great alertness in the painter: he had to be able to put his ideas into effect rapidly on an extensive scale. . . . This is [an art which attached] particular importance to delicate rapidity of touch. . . . These pictures were not intended to be seen in isolation from the rest of their wall and room . . . [and they] were intended to be seen in a more subdued light [than is provided by museums or the present ruined roofless houses of the two towns]. . . .

The more important compositions were derived from Greek originals executed at some time or other during the preceding three centuries.[3]

The colours used were plain earth (ochre), and minerals (carbonate of copper), and dyes of animal or vegetable origin: 'Pompeian' reds, blues, greens, yellows and blacks were used. (Black was lustrous, and regarded as particularly luxurious, and employed for the best rooms.) When applied to the walls, these pigments were supplemented by soapy limestone and a bonding medium; and then the finished surface was polished with wax to increase durability and brightness: repeated polishings gave the walls a glossy brilliance which greatly helped to make the rooms less gloomy.

Sometimes, too, Greek masterpieces or Hellenistic originals, or other notable pictures, were removed from their original settings and transplanted, being placed, very often, in suitably situated wooden panels (*pinakes*). Cicero mentions placing high-class paintings in a 'good light', and Vitruvius mentions picture-galleries (*pinacothecoe*) as part of the proper domestic arrangements of a nobleman. One must assume that such pictures often aroused comment and discussion among their viewers.[4]

An outstanding masterpiece from Pompeii is the so-called 'Lost Ram'[5] painted after the middle of the first century AD, and apparently of what is known as the Fourth (Last) Pompeian Style (Figure 29).[6] Most mural paintings at Pompeii were made and placed as carefully judged items in the overall decoration of a room, but in the case of the 'Lost Ram' we are obliged to dispense with any knowledge of this factor, because we do not know what house it came from, though it was evidently the centrepiece of a wall-panel in some house or other. That is to say, the picture has to be judged on its merits. And they are high.

The painting displays a landscape – a fashionable theme for artists of the period[7] – within which we see an idealized rustic shrine, located within rocky scenery containing trees. On a rock to the right stands a shepherd, and on another rock, to the left, there is another pair of figures, one of which is a statue.

In the foreground a man is guiding or pushing a ram or goat, covered with long hair, towards the shrine, as if for sacrifice. That is to say, despite the general tranquillity of the scene (which reveals other quietly grazing animals), there is evidence of tension. The animal, it would seem, had run away from the flock, but has been discovered again, and been brought back, reluctantly and defiantly, to its final fate.

The painting is clever: clearly the work of a master of impressionism. The goat and herdsman are represented by a few well-chosen brush-strokes. A dark colour is employed, with a paucity of highlights. And by this means the figures of the man and the goat are projected like shadows upon the walls of the shrine, which are light-coloured, with a preference for whitish grey and pale purple, and a matt yellow-brown tone in the foreground. The rocks in the background seem to start dark grey, turn to purple-white, and finally gleam in purple-pink, as if the last rays of the sun were striking the mountainside. Subtle variations of mood and accent were attained within the framework of tradition.

The paintings executed during the last decades of the life of Pompeii, Herculaneum and Stabiae show an amazing diversity of bold, fluent and skilfully graded colours. . . . Infusing a fresh animation into the traditional pastoral landscapes of shrines and trees, the new impressionistic ideas produce masterpieces like *The Lost Ram*. In this picture the two figures, man and ram, appear like shadows in front of the light walls of the sanctuary, against a romantic landscape of wild gorges and caverns.[8]

There has been a good deal of discussion about the social status and prestige

Figure 29 Painting known as 'The Lost Ram' from Pompeii, AD 60s or 70s. Museo Archeologico Nazionale, Naples.

Opinions of the wall-paintings at Pompeii and Herculaneum and Stabiae, preserved by the eruption of Mount Vesuvius in AD 79 which overwhelmed the towns, have varied sharply; some call them good, others bad. Bear in mind, first, that they were made to fill a specific place in a specific room, often with a view to seemingly enlarging its dimensions; second, that many of the best were copied from originals by skilful frescoists (Romans, Greeks or near easterners) who had to work quickly. We do not know what room the 'Lost Ram' was designed for, what house it came from, nor what original, if any, its painter (whoever he was) copied. It has to stand, therefore, on its own merits.

94

of the painters of such pictures, of whom we know the names of quite a number – though not, unfortunately, of the painter of the 'Lost Ram'. Many of the artists were evidently Greek or Greek-trained. It does not seem that theirs was a particularly degraded or despised profession – though, like other arts, it was not an occupation for the upper classes.

MUMMY-PAINTINGS

The other truly important movement in the paintings of the Roman empire is that of the mummy-'portrait' artists in Egypt,[9] whose work ranges in date from the early first century BC until the fourth century AD. Most of these paintings come from the cemeteries of Moeris (the Fayum oasis), 60 miles south of Cairo, where a lake is linked by canal to the Nile. There are labels, however, which indicate that certain dead people from Philadelphia (Darb Gerze), in the north-eastern Fayum, were buried beside the Nile itself.[10]

These 'portraits' replaced, to a large extent, the plaster masks that had been used in Hellenistic Egypt. What makes them notable is their artists' capacity to display what seem to be the characters of the men and women (prominent here, Figure 30) whose dead bodies are mummified. Attention is lavished on their facial features, but little on their costumes. They are lifelike images. They make us delight in the people represented – even if we are left in little doubt about their social status, which (like that of the men and women represented at Palmyra) was pretty elevated – and we are inclined to feel sympathy with them and to like them. Sometimes they remind us of someone we know, someone we have encountered during our daily life. Sometimes they make us smile, because they look a little vulgar, and their vulgarity is reproduced with such skill.

These mummy-paintings, then, look lifelike. Throughout the first, second and third centuries AD, their luminous highlights and sharply contrasted shadows give forth a conspicuous effect of three-dimensional plasticity, which adds to the lifelike effect. Reference has already been made to the apparent individuality of the countenances. Yet, all the same, the identical word of caution that was offered in connection with the sculptures of Palmyra is necessary here. For it would appear to be improbable that the people represented by these paintings actually sat for them while they were still alive. And this improbability, despite the insertion of personal details, makes one suspect a degree of fictitiousness, or at least of idealization. Furthermore, there is a similarity in the penetrative eyes and other facial features that keep on occurring on a number of these mummy-paintings. And old age is rarely rendered (one can scarcely suppose that all those 'portrayed' had died young). Certainly there is a leaning towards the inherited Greco-Roman tradition of realistic iconography. Yet one wonders whether these heads are *really* portraits: or are they, despite their vividness, somewhat standard images of the dead? Or had they been, after all, made while the subjects were alive – but still presumably not from personal portrayal? Whatever the answers to these questions, the heads are meant to be images of people who will be resurrected for eternity.

Figure 30 Painting of young woman's head on a mummy-panel from Antinoupolis (Sheikh Ibada) in Egypt. Later first century AD. Institute of Arts, Detroit.

The few portraits produced at Pompeii and Herculaneum were nothing compared to the flood of heads painted on the panels which were inserted in mummy-cases in Egypt, and especially around Lake Moeris (the Fayum) and Antinoupolis.

This custom, which started in the first century AD, continued throughout the imperial epoch, producing heads both of men and of women – to whose life in the empire, at least at this somewhat elevated level of society, the heads bear unusual testimony. Many could be illustrated, but I have chosen a fairly early woman's head.

These mummy-'portraits' are executed, for the most part, upon a thin piece of wood inserted in the mummy-case at the head of the body, or, less frequently, upon the linen shroud in which the body was swathed. The painting was done either straight on to the wood, or on a specially prepared basis of gypsum plaster. The pigments were made more liquid by the admixture of water, with the addition of some sort of gum or glue (tempera, with egg white as a binding medium) or of beeswax (encaustic, used especially for the earliest paintings: the pigments were pulverized in hot wax applied by heated irons). And the colours thus produced possess a special, rich and brilliant quality, which seems a little garish at times – but often looks like a forecast of modern oil painting.

Egypt was not otherwise notable, in Roman times, for the quality of its art. But these heads do a lot to make up the deficiency. Besides, they are almost our sole surviving evidence (except for a few isolated examples from elsewhere) for the examination of ancient 'portrait'-painting. And they make a remarkable impact, not only because they seem to anticipate our own age, but because, despite the queries relating to generalization raised above, their human interest is so strong. In the best of these 'portraits', or 'heads' as we had better call them, the countenances are captivatingly depicted, the highlighted drawing is sharp and graceful, and the general level of craftsmanship is high – even if we rarely have the feeling of first-class mastery, since the speed and scale with which these paintings were turned out look like the performances of hard-worked men out to make money, rather than the leisurely output of a talented artist.

One wonders how and where these men learned to paint plastically treated heads of this type. There seems, as I have suggested, to have been a double tradition, of Romanized Hellenism and Egyptian Pharaonic art. Relevant to the latter – not altogether surprisingly, since these families were sufficiently Egyptian to adopt the burial customs of the country in which they lived and died – are paintings on linen which show the dead person with Anubis (escort of the dead) and Osiris (judge in the eternal kingdom)[11] – although most of the names of the dead persons that have come down to us are Greek. The paintings are difficult to date, but some guidance is provided by the hair-styles of the women.

One of the paintings, attributable to AD 130–60, is in the Detroit Institute of Arts (Figure 29).[12] It is highly expressive, though, as we have seen, there is reason to wonder whether it is really, in the fullest sense, a portrait.

THE EVIDENCE AND ITS SURVIVAL

So there were two important developments in the history of painting that have to be traced back to the Roman empire, and both have left evidence for our inspection owing to special circumstances. In the first case, these circumstances were provided by the eruption of Mount Vesuvius, which preserved so many of the houses and murals of Pompeii, Herculaneum and Stabiae. These paintings, of such diversity that they have been divided (as mentioned above) into four styles, are a treasure-house of information regarding the evolution of the pictorial art in the first centuries BC and AD. Some of the pictures are copies of well-known Greek masterpieces, but others appear to be original; we do not, for the most part, know who the painters were, but perhaps they were of Greek or eastern origin, attracted as immigrants to Rome by the better financial possibilities there.[13]

The second significant development that we are able to trace comprises the mummy-portraits, or rather painted heads, of Egypt. And here the special circumstances that have led to their preservation are provided by the dry sand of that country which has acted as a preservative. The heads display to us what regional traditions, combined with Hellenism and stimulated by Romanism, could achieve; and they offer a new warning against simply identifying the Roman empire and its art with Rome.

INTERIOR DECORATION

It must not be thought, however, that Egypt was the only province of the Roman empire in which painting flourished, even if surviving specimens from elsewhere are so rare.

> Roman styles of interior decoration also became part of monumental art in Palestine and other provinces of the Roman empire, and current research is revealing, almost on a daily basis, new examples of provincial material that has remained all but unknown until now. . . . Wall-paintings in the provinces reflect a combination of local styles, with their strong Hellenistic influences, and the styles of decoration developed in Rome and Campania. . . . The influence of Roman styles of painting and stucco-work became evident in every locality that was part of the Roman empire; beautiful examples have been found in the various provinces. . . . In paintings of the second and early third centuries, the majority of mythological compositions appear on tombs. The time – the third century in particular – was one of change and unrest, when people searched for a more personal religion and turned their thoughts to the afterlife. These paintings and their mythological themes reflect the aspirations of the period. A number of surviving examples from the Levant illustrate the changes that affected styles of representation: a divergence from the tradition of illusionistic representations and a new emphasis on the use of large-scale figured murals occupying much of the wall-surface.[14]

STUCCO

Decorative painting was eked out by stucco (Figure 31), which thus played a part in the artistic output of the Roman empire.[15] It provided low-relief designs

Figure 31 Stucco at Stabiae in Campania.

Examples of stucco decoration in low relief can be seen in many parts of the Roman empire, and particularly at Rome itself, and in the prosperous houses of Campania. 'For good material reasons', observes R. E. M. Wheeler (1964: 213 f.), 'the primary centre of plasterwork in the ancient world was Alexandria. The coastline for many miles to the west of the city is a great bank of gypsum or "plaster" which shines like sunlit snow against the deep ultramarine of the sea. From the foundation of Alexandria onwards this ready and abundant material was used extensively by the Ptolemaic sculptors as a partial substitute for the traditional white marble, which does not occur naturally in Egypt and was a costly import.'

in plaster. The technique had been known in ancient Egypt, and then in the last centuries BC the Ptolemies had employed stucco as a substitute for imported marble. The primary centre of such plaster-work, at that time, was still Alexandria, which employed the gypsum plaster that was to be found over an area of many miles west of the city.

The Romans began to make use of this medium from the early first century BC, describing it as *opus albarium*. Stucco-work was undertaken in and near Rome, and became a prominent feature of private houses and baths at Pompeii where it covered walls around the city. Stucco-work appeared all over the empire, and in easterly lands outside it as well. Furthermore,

> amongst other uses, plaster became the staple medium for the manufacture of the careful models from which, usually by casting and with subsequent chasing, much . . . silverwork . . . was produced.[16]

TEXTILE-WORK

Another art was that of textile-work, particularly on bedspreads. Although the evidence has almost totally disappeared, fragments have survived from Egypt, notably a few depicting mythological scenes.

The second-century scholar Pollux of Naucratis suggests to us how much we have missed owing to the disappearance of every ancient bedspread or counter-pane. He calls them delicate, well-woven, glistening, beautifully coloured, adorned with many flowers, covered with ornaments, purple, dark green, scarlet, violet, rich with scarlet blooms, purple-bordered, shot with gold, embroidered with figures of animals, gleaming with stars.[17]

12

MOSAICS

Mosaics made of small, equal-sized cubes of coloured stones and marbles (*opus tessellatum*), arranged in . . . lines [not always straight] in their beds of cement, became gradually known to the Greek world during the decades following the conquests of Alexander III the Great in the fourth century BC. Probably the idea came from the east, although Sicilian origin has also been suggested. The predominant conception was reminiscent of textiles [see end of Chapter 11] – although now the idea was transferred to a more permanent medium.

The mosaic, or its pictorial part, was thought of as a sort of rug let into the middle of the floor-space of a room, this central panel being known as the *emblema*. Or it could be like a mat beside the door. . . .

The mosaic . . . became one of the most characteristic and successful arts of the Roman world. . . . People began to form a different interpretation of what mosaics ought to be like. The floor was now envisaged as a unified space, to be covered all over by a mosaic, which thus resembled a carpet rather than a rug or mat.[1]

And then, after some time, the inhabitants of the Roman world habitually began to use mosaics for the sides and tops of interior arches, apses and walls; whereas, in classical times, they had chiefly been employed for floors.

Seven major stylistic groups of these floor-mosaics have been identified, existing in different geographical parts of the Roman world. North Africa was one of the seven regions, and the thousands of tessellated floors preserved by its dry soil include some of the empire's most significant mosaic work, bringing provincial and local styles to the fore, intermingled with Roman and Carthaginian influences, with results that are sometimes a little crude – for example, owing to their artists' ignorance or disregard of perspective – but are always full of decorative value.

Private houses in North Africa quite often possessed mosaic floors. Many of these depict scenes from daily life, and are, indeed, one of our principal sources of information regarding the lives that the people of the country lived at that time. There are other North African mosaics too, notably those depicting mythological events, which were evidently copies of well-known Greek or eastern paintings. But a number remain which, even if influenced by coastwise travelling Alexandrian craftsmen, are still relatively unconnected with any such models, or with any other Greek or Roman prototype. They display local scenes in a lively spirit of naturalism that may be purely regional or may owe something to the artistic traditions of the ancient east. The outstanding merits of the tapestry-like mosaics of this African school – which extended its influence as far as Italy – can be summed up, both in regard to choice of subject-matter and in technical handling, in three fashions: as a sympathetic realism in the depiction of human figures, a capacity for vigour, and a sensuous liking for colour.[2]

Some of the results are to be seen in the Alaoui (Bardo) Museum at Tunis, which is unequalled in its collection of mosaics of Roman times. These include ambitious figure subjects and landscapes. And some of these mosaics are especially informative owing to their depiction of houses and palaces, and of agricultural scenes. The mosaics in this museum have been collected from a considerable number of Tunisian sites, and are frequently of an unusually high quality of workmanship.

Although they are often hard to date, it seems to have been Septimius Severus (193–211), himself a North African, who pushed the technique, as well as other branches of African art, into changes resulting in a new style of greater competence and lavishness. But one famous mosaic is considerably later, having been made in *c.* 380–400. This shows the mansion of Dominus Julius at Carthage (Figure 32).[3] The centrepiece of the mosaic is an extensive villa, turreted at the corners, so that it is a blend of a residential house and a fortress: the living quarters are situated on the first floor (behind a splendid *loggia*) so as to provide a measure of protection in case of attack, during these disturbed years of the late fourth century. An arched entrance gives access to the spacious ground floor, which no doubt contained numerous additional rooms and was probably flanked by a courtyard. Behind this principal building are dome-roofed private baths, partially hidden in the mosaic.

Around the villa is a park, and on two sides is shown a hunting expedition led by the master of the house. The upper and lower sections of the mosaic display scenes of life on the estate. And each corner is occupied by one of the four Seasons, a familiar theme of mosaicists which is here incorporated into the household scenes.

As a portrait of rural life the mosaic is redolent of the *douceur de vivre* that was still possible for the rich. The house is surrounded by a pleasure garden; there are cereal crops and olive trees, domestic animals and poultry, huntsmen, servants and farm labourers. The master, in the time he cares to spare from the pursuit of game, watches over his domain; his wife, fashionably dressed in spite of exile from Carthage, gazes at herself in a mirror. Estates like this one were beginning to develop into self-

Figure 32 Mosaic of the house of Dominus Julius, found at Carthage. Third–fourth centuries AD. Alaoui (Bardo) Museum, Tunis.

The art of the floor mosaic evolved enormously, throughout the Roman empire. The tradition remained Greek and Hellenistic, but regional diversities were marked. It proved strongest and most lasting in North Africa. And there, at a number of centres, specific regional characteristics developed. One type of mosaic represented aspects of the daily life of the area's landowners, and also displayed their houses, in considerable detail: this mosaic of Dominus Julius, and his villa, is from a house in Carthage. Perhaps the mosaicist was a North African.

contained communities. . . . The poor grew poorer; but the rich grew richer.[4]

Not many of the elements in the Dominus Julius mosaic are new, but they are collected here in such a way as to constitute a novelty.[5]

* * *

Mosaics have survived because they are better equipped to do so than, say, paintings – they have been described as 'paintings for eternity'. Owing to this large-scale survival they deserve special investigation as examples of the art of the Roman empire.

Usually they formed simple decorative patterns. Sometimes it has been said that these rarely deserve to be called truly artistic. But this view has been contested:

Only blinkered theorists will deny that some masterpieces of this kind are expressive and impressive works of art. . . . Mosaic usually represents the dominant aspects of the political, intellectual, social and economic conditions of an epoch. . . . Today this ancient art is, in fact, one of the most contemporary as well, for, by its very nature, it has close affinities with modern styles.[6]

Although abundant enough in Italy, such mosaics exhibit, within other parts of the Roman empire, stylistic differences corresponding to the different regions in which they have been found. In the present book, North Africa has been selected as the country in which the art reached its most prolific and peculiar development. As always, we are not told who the artists were. But probably they were Africans, though they might have come from elsewhere, like the sculptors at Lepcis Magna (Lebda) in Libya, who seem to have originated from Aphrodisias in Caria. And we do know of one mosaicist who was a Greek, namely Dioscurides of Samos, the signatory of two mosaics at Pompeii of the first century BC, offering scenes from the Athenian New Comedy (which are no doubt copies of Greek paintings).[7] Such sparse indications are invaluable because they form rare exceptions to our ignorance about who the artists and architects of the Roman empire were.

13

COINS AND MEDALLIONS

THE ROMAN COINAGE

Alexander Pope accurately saw the significance of the Roman coinage:

> Ambition sigh'd: she found it vain to trust
> The faithless Column and the crumbling Bust;
> Huge moles, whose shadows stretched from shore to shore,
> Their ruins ruin'd, and their place no more!
> Convinc'd, she now constructs her vast design,
> And all her Triumphs shrinks into a Coin. . . .
> A small Euphrates thro' the piece is rolled
> And little Eagles wave their wings in gold.[1]

Both the obverses and reverses of the coins played their part. Of the former, I remarked:

Roman coinage, like Greek coinage, was intended to be looked at, and was looked at. . . . Coins were more portable than busts, and more widely distributed. So, for the dissemination of the ruler's features, the fullest possible use was made of the coinage. Coin-portraits had their share of the veneration accorded to imperial statues; for the coinage was itself under divine patronage, and was, in due course, even described as 'sacred'.

The Roman authorities, and the artists whom they employed, varied the coin-portraits of an emperor as continually and skilfully as they varied his portrait-busts. He appears in turn as war-lord, priest, far-gazing semi-divine potentate, unpretentiously bare-headed Italian magistrate. And sometimes his actual features were drastically idealized and rejuvenated. . . . So for hundreds of years the mint poured out a remarkable series of successive imperial faces, intended to impress the personalities and glories of the rulers on their people.[2]

But the reverses too were significant; Marcus Aurelius (AD 161–80) alone issued no fewer than 1,500 different reverse-types.

The Roman rulers of the world [did not] fail to notice that a coin has two sides. Their subjects were not generally fastidious enough to appreciate great artistry in the reverse-types of their coinage. But this deficiency was counterbalanced by their susceptibility to news – and where could they find this news better than on the coinage? So it is with news that its reverses are crammed. And, of course, this news is edifying: it points an imperial moral, and it was selected at a high level. . . . There were stringent conventions and traditions governing the choice of coin-types. . . . [But] what is most surprising to us is the immense variety of these reverse-designs. . . . As evidence for the ancient world, the coins deserve comparison with the ancient writers themselves.[3]

In particular, the coins were used by successive emperors – who were well aware that the imperial gold and silver issues penetrated to every corner of the Roman world – in order to stress their personal interests and predilections. This was especially true of Hadrian (AD 117–38), who went from place to place not only to keep the army in a state of skilled readiness, but also because of his own innate curiosity, and because of his desire to elevate the provinces into entities enjoying their own pride, their own rights, their local spirits and traditions. It was his wish, in fact, to elevate them into partners rather than merely conquered possessions.

Hadrian . . . was the greatest imperial traveller that the world has ever known; most of his reign was spent in a series of royal tours. Himself a provincial from Spain [Italica], he thought of the empire as 'no mere system of dependencies, but a living organism, alive in all its parts, each sharing, each enjoying the personal interest and care of emperors'. On an unparalleled series of coins he commemorated his own visits to no less than eighteen provinces or territories. . . . This theme of 'Adventus' remained an important one for centuries. . . . Another series shows Hadrian's 'restoration', by beneficent measures, of twelve countries. . . . On another great series he honoured, without fear, the provincial armies. . . . Yet another group of coins, issued at the same date, quite simply commemorates certain lands by name. . . . He was not afraid to suggest that the provinces should themselves help in their own defence: so *Britannia* displays her own national costume and shield [Figure 33].[4]

The present book, however, is more about art than about imperial ambitions and propaganda, and the artistic qualities of Roman coins must not be forgotten.

Coins, considered as an art, possess a strong and indeed growing claim upon the keen eyes and sympathetic interest of those who love what is

Figure 33 Sestertii of Hadrian (AD 134–8) celebrating AEGVPTOS and MAVRETANIA, who is personified as a figure with headdress and standard. From a sale catalogue.

The emperor's bureau issued the coins which went from Rome and other imperial mints all over the provinces, and beyond the frontiers as well. And fine portraits made his appearance and his family's well known throughout every province. Reverse designs were numerous and constantly changing (in marked contrast to the coinages of our own time, when TV, radio and the press keep the public informed). In the reign of Hadrian (117–38), these reverse designs were often concentrated upon the various provinces, which received novel numismatic honours reflecting contemporary imperial views of the autonomous dignity of the various parts of the Roman empire.

beautiful. Viewed simply as a sequence of artistic creation . . . the coinage of the western world presents a fine and consistent continuity, combined with a perfection in survival, which perhaps no other art-form could surpass. Judged from the narrower, if more exacting, standpoint of purely technical achievement the record is scarcely less impressive. . . .

At nearly all times coins have shown directness of appeal, essential humanity, and a quality which, falling happily short of sophistication, rises far above the merely simple. For the art expressed in coinage is a pre-eminently social art. The first purpose of coins is to serve as a social commodity.... They have at most periods reflected the spirit of their time with a bright and curiously spontaneous fidelity....

If, in spite of this, the art-history of coinage has been to some extent neglected in the past while that of painting or sculpture or architecture has thrived, a reason is possibly to be found in the very small scale of the coins themselves.[5]

In addition, however, to these imperial gold and silver issues,[6] there were the local bronze coins of the various cities, mainly in the east.

Under Augustus ... not less than three hundred towns in the Roman empire struck their own bronze coinage. Later this number considerably increased.... No historian can effectively study any Roman emperor's reign unless he has a good knowledge of the local coinages issued in all parts of the empire during that reign.[7]

The *aes* coinage throughout the empire provides an extraordinary wealth of material for the study of provincial art. It includes a series of documents which outdoes all other contemporary evidence in extent and probably also in value: this value is enhanced by the unselfconscious carelessness with which many of the types are executed.... Good and bad alike bear the stamp of regional influences.

[But] many of the criteria for regional attribution are based on considerations too intangible for description.... Spanish [and Gallic] mints provide examples of native influences.... In Africa the issues ... show an unmistakable and persistent individuality which bears witness to a firm fusion of the three principal racial elements (Roman, Libyan, Punic) to form a homogeneous graphic art.... Characteristic of the Balkan provinces is a mild, neat, uninspired style, of which both Greek and Roman constituents can be noted, the former usually predominating....

The province of Asia is sufficiently extensive and variegated for its several regions to have characteristics that enable a fairly close attribution of uncertain coins within the province.... The remaining parts of Asia Minor mostly have styles which are distinguishable at least within certain limits....

Research would be most rewarded in the Syrian region, where numismatic styles are as unusual, mixed and obscure as those in other mediums.[8]

Something was said, in that passage, about the artistic characteristics of these local issues, but the subject is one on which, so far, research has been somewhat lacking. An exception to this neglect, however, is provided by Cornelius C. Vermeule III, who has written as follows:

Vignettes found nowhere else in Roman numismatic art begin in the series of Greek imperial coins.... It was really under the Flavians, particularly Vespasian and Domitian, that Greek imperial coins broke from their Hellenistic origins and became a clearly defined part of the Roman Empire in the East and West.... The high point of Greek imperial coins begins under Commodus (180–92) and extends through Severus Alexander (222–35).... If the obverses of the biggest and widest Greek imperial coins range from traditional medallic relief to hairy flatness, the reverses dazzle us by their variety of messages and complexity of compositions.... The reign of the young emperor Gordianus III (238–44) marked a transition of sorts ... to the imaginative confusion of the last quarter-century of Greek imperial coins in Greece and Asia Minor.

It must have occurred to a large group of [second-century] urban magistrates and their gifted die-designers ... that their regional and local coinages offered one of the few latitudes for individual expression in the Roman empire.... Imperial portraits were imaginative, not so much in their iconography as in their sometimes wild regional styles.... Roman imperial coins gave urban die-designers models from mints in the Latin West and the Greek East. Emperors were often present in the eastern Mediterranean, where their features could be recorded. Finally, when all else was unavailable, sketches and models must have been prepared from recollections and educated guesswork, the way modern police departments produce composite pictures of wanted criminals.... [And] cities of the Greek world celebrated limited events dear to their hearts.... There are strong regional styles in the urban coinages of northern Greece and Asia Minor.... Asia Minor is always the touchstone of Greek imperial numismatic art.... Compositions circulated back and forth between Italy, Greece, Asia Minor and the East.... In contrast to the Roman imperial coinages from the mint of Rome and its subsidiaries, there is, of course, much greater latitude for stylistic variation in the Greek imperial issues with their multitude of cities and regions.[9]

MEDALLIONS

In addition to Roman coins, there were coin-like pieces of various kinds, usually of some size, that we are accustomed to describe as 'medallions'. These were intended, for the most part, for presentation by the emperor, or members of his court, to individuals, for instance at New Year and other ceremonials. On these pieces, portraiture is even more effective than on coins, and the reverses offer room for complex and elaborate scenes, replete with religious, allegorical, or traditionalistic allusions.

The production of medallions in all metals increased during the Antonine

Figure 34 Bronze (*aes*) medallion of Antoninus Pius (AD 138–61), showing the walls of Lavinium (Pratica Mare), with a statue of its mythical founder Aeneas, carrying his father Anchises. One of a series of pieces issued in advance of the ninth centenary of Rome (AD 148). Bibliothèque Nationale, Paris.

Especially from the second century AD, the imperial government produced medallions, in all metals but particularly brass, bronze and copper, to commemorate special occasions, and to distribute as gifts. Some or most were of considerable size, which made it possible to present fine portraits and complex, artistic reverses. Like the coins, they conveyed imperial points of view. Thus this *aes* medallion reacted against the internationalism of the philhellenic Hadrian by emphasizing ancient and traditional Italian themes, particularly in preparation for the centenary mentioned above.

period, reaching its peak of quantity and quality under Commodus (180–92); though as times went on the types had become fussier and heavier.[10] As it happens, the best-known and most spectacular medallions are somewhat earlier. They are the large *aes* pieces which began to be issued at the beginning of the second century AD. These were issued to commemorate special occasions.

> Medallions are pieces struck by the emperor for special or solemn commemoration and primarily and specifically intended for presentation or distribution as individual personal gifts, any idea of their circulation as currency being either wholly absent or, at the most, quite secondary and subordinate.[11]

Among these propagandist medallions, a group of issues of Antoninus Pius is outstanding. It is the group of his bronze medallions issued in advance of the nine-hundredth anniversary of the foundation of Rome (Figure 34).[12] Full of historical, mythological and artistic interest, these pieces display the intensity of Antoninus' antiquarian interests, and his resolve that similar interests should figure strongly in the official circles around him. The medallions provide evidence for the extent of his preparations, in consequence of this resolve, for the solemn anniversary occasion of Rome's ninth centenary. And they reveal the manner in which he pronounced that this was to be a national event of the first importance.

The cities of the empire, too, produced artistically important *aes* medallions of their own, especially in Asia Minor.[13]

* * *

The artistic quality of the imperial portraits on Roman coins and medallions has sometimes been appreciated, and rightly so. They deserve (as was the intention of their designers) to be set alongside the portrait-busts of emperors and their families which have justly gained so much admiration. And in a few cases, though not universally, the aesthetic merits of reverses have been recognized (it must be admitted that although these merits are sometimes high, they are not always so). The reverses of the local, Greek imperial medallions are also, on occasion, of considerable artistic merit; though much work still remains to be done on this theme.

14

GEMS AND JEWELS

CAMEOS

The large Roman output of jewellery included massive cameos, the earliest dating from the first century BC, and probably first made in Egypt, from which craftsmen went to Italy, where the bulk of the demand was to be found. These cameos reached their climax in the early part of the first century AD, after which they soon faded away. Although cameos in high relief were made out of various materials, including amethyst and chalcedony, the usual material was sardonyx, which consists of alternate layers of brown sard and white onyx, and was cut down vertically in order to create the required designs.[1]

Many of these cameos displayed imperial types, thus serving the same sort of propagandist purpose as large-scale public reliefs and medallions (before the latter came into any substantial existence). They include such manifestations of the Augustan and Julio-Claudian imperial spirit as the Grand Camée de France at the Louvre in Paris, the Blacas Cameo in the British Museum and the Gemma Augustea in the Kunsthistorisches Museum at Vienna (Figure 35).

This last-named piece measures 10 by nearly 7½ inches, and is made of onyx.[2] Its brown layer has a bluish tinge, and the rest is as usual white. The cameo is nowadays incomplete on its upper left extremity, where there was originally at least one additional figure. The field is divided into two parts, both crammed with imperial symbolism. In the lower register are figures of defeated barbarians, displayed in conjunction with Roman soldiers occupied in the erection of a trophy. The upper part of the cameo shows the emperor's adopted son (and eventual successor) Tiberius, directly above the trophy pole, stepping out of his chariot after celebrating a Triumph – probably in AD 12, in honour of his victory over Germans and Pannonians. As for Augustus himself, he is seen seated, with a conscious echo of Jupiter, beside Roma personified. He is waiting to receive the victorious Tiberius.

This design, replete with cool classicism, brings together the commander on the battlefield (Tiberius, with his trophy), and the ultimate, imperial source and beneficiary of his victory, the powerful, ever-fortunate Augustus. The scene is

Figure 35 The great imperial cameos date from the first quarter or half of the first century AD. This Gemma Augustea at Vienna, a piece of onyx measuring about $8\frac{1}{2}$ by $7\frac{1}{4}$ inches, portrays the deification of Augustus.

The emperor is throned with the goddess Roma (Livia?) at his side. Above, his symbol of a capricorn; at his feet, the eagle of Jupiter. On the left, a triumphal chariot, from which steps Tiberius. The charioteer is Victory, and at the horses' heads stands Germanicus. On the right, Ge (the inhabited earth, placing a wreath on the emperor's head), Tellus and Oceanus. Below, Roman soldiers set up a trophy, round which are grouped barbarian prisoners. Designer, executant and recipient are unknown; it may have originated in the eastern Mediterranean area.

derived from some lost composition, Roman but probably of Hellenistic inspiration.[3]

Although we can detect that the onyx of which the cameo is made is Arabian, we do not know, as is so often the case, who designed the cameo and made it. But it is worth recording that the most famous gem-cutter of the Augustan age, a man even known to literature, was Dioscurides of Aegeae (Ayaş) in Cilicia, who created a seal-stone for Augustus.[4]

PERSONAL JEWELLERY

Personal jewellery, of course, proliferated during the Roman empire, and does not, on the whole, represent a very high art, although the technical skill which was employed in order to display these rich materials is unmistakable.

Expensive jewellery is to be seen on the ladies sculpted at Palmyra and on the mummy-portraits of Egypt, and this eastern geographical emphasis is not fortuitous, since Alexandria as well as Antioch, the two principal centres of Hellenistic jewellery, continued their traditional work in this field, although many of their jewellers were attracted to Rome. Much jewellery, often of Egyptian or Syrian make, was also to be found further east, notably in Parthia and Mampsis in Nabataean Arabia (Kornub in the Negev) – which produced ear-rings made by five generations of jewellers (Figure 36).[5] And Syrian jewel-workers accompanied merchants from their country who went not only to Rome but also to France and Spain, and apparently even Sarmatia.[6]

Much of this jewellery was simply a continuation of what had been fashionable in the Hellenistic epoch. As time went on, however, other influences increasingly made themselves felt; by the fourth or fifth centuries AD, for example, more and more emphasis was placed on stones for their own sake.

*   *   *

Gems and jewels may form part of a minor and not very highly considered art, but the Gemma Augustea and other pieces like it show how cameos could be used in the same way as other artistic media to impress the personalities of the emperors and their families upon selected recipients. Such efforts were not always in the best of taste, but they demanded ability on the artists' part. Who were these artists? Once again, we do not know, apart from our accidental knowledge of Dioscurides of Aegeae, though we can surmise that they, like him, were Greeks or easterners who had come to Rome in search of the superior patronage that was to be found there.

Personal jewellery overrode geographical ties and considerations, since a rich or well-connected woman wanted to wear it, wherever she might be, and wherever it came from.

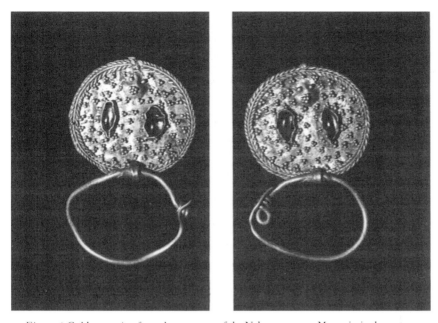

Figure 36 Golden ear-ring from the cemetery of the Nabataean town Mampsis, in the eastern Negev; perhaps made in Alexandria. First or second century AD. Collection of Dr Avraham Negev.

In every province of the Roman empire, as well as at Rome itself, the wealthier women wore expensive gold and silver jewellery, combined with precious and semi-precious stones; witness the mummy-heads of Egypt (Figure 30) and the sculptural heads of deceased women at Palmyra (Figure 4) which are loaded with jewels.

Rome, Alexandria and Antioch were among the principal centres. A particularly rich find-spot for Roman jewellery is Mampsis.

I5

SILVER

The display of gold and silver among private citizens in the form of
jewellery and plate was the natural counterpart of imperial magnificence. . . . Close attention had to be paid to the production of gold and
silver within the empire, to ownership of the areas of production . . . and
to the recovery by taxation and confiscation of as much gold and silver as
possible. . . .

The surviving hoards of plate, enriched in recent years by important
finds . . . can be accepted confidently both as illustrations of the best
product of Roman silversmiths, and also as the possessions of the more
wealthy and influential members of imperial society. . . .

The largest number of discoveries have been made in areas where the
danger was greatest, on the borders of the empire.[1]

Gold plate was in demand among the Roman rich, as it had been among
prosperous Hellenistic Greeks. Silver plate, too, was owned by wealthy Roman
families, and could include large and highly decorated dishes, salvers, bowls and
jugs. Many of them came from the east: notably two plates in the Augusta
Rauricorum (Kaiseraugst) Treasure, which were made at Thessalonica (Salonica)
and Naissus (Niş).

When the various peoples beyond the frontiers started dangerously overrun-
ning Roman imperial territory in the fourth century AD, many of these well-
provided owners in threatened lands buried their silverware underground, and
were never able afterwards to recover what they had buried, so that it has come
to light again in modern times and can once again be seen. One of the most
significant of these hoards, from an artistic point of view is the Mildenhall
Treasure, found at West Row, two miles north-west of the English village of
Mildenhall, near the remains of a fourth-century Roman building. It is conjectured (on the basis of a Greek graffito inscription *eutheriou* on the backs of two
silver platters in the hoard) that much or all of the Treasure might have
belonged to the Armenian Eutherius, a high pagan official of the Emperor
Julian the Apostate (361–3) and that Eutherius could have given it to the
Christian Lupicinus, who had served in Egypt and Gaul, from which he was

Figure 37 The Great Dish from Mildenhall, Suffolk. British Museum.
We owe the survival of some of the finest late imperial silverware to the troubled conditions of the fourth century AD, which caused landowners to bury their treasures for safety. Among a number of finds, the Mildenhall (Suffolk) Treasure is one of the most important. It includes the Great Dish, almost 2 feet in diameter, weighing more than 18 pounds. Around the central mask of Oceanus is an inner frieze of Nereids and fantastic sea-creatures. The outer frieze portrays a Bacchic debauch.

sent to Britain (in 360).[2] The 360s seem a suitable time for all such objects to be buried and hidden, since that was a time when Pictish and Scottish raiders from Caledonia were harrassing the coasts and borders of Roman Britain.

Altogether, the Mildenhall hoard consists of over thirty items of silver tableware – platters and bowls, and spoons and goblets; most of them are lavishly decorated. Among them – the most remarkable object to survive from Roman Britain – is the Great Dish (Figure 37), which measures nearly 2 feet across and weighs more than 18 pounds. The central feature of its elaborate relief decoration is a frontal head of Oceanus, with dolphins in his hair. Surrounding this head is a circular frieze of Nereids and fantastic animals of the sea. The outer frieze displays a Dionysian orgy, and depicts the god Dionysus (Bacchus) himself with a panther, an intoxicated Hercules propped up by two satyrs, other satyrs dancing, and Maenads doing the same, and Silenus and Pan.[3]

This inclusion of motifs of a pagan character[4] may not mean much from a theological point of view: for the pieces found in the Treasure were not intended to have any religious significance, and even if its owner was a Christian (which, as we have seen, he may or may not have been) he would scarcely have had these magnificent pieces of silver melted down merely because of this pagan decoration.[5]

If rich women everywhere in the Roman world wanted to wear jewellery, rich men everywhere wanted to display fine silver on their tables; and when 'barbarian' enemies became threatening along the fringes of the empire, they buried it underground, as has been said. But it may be repeated that most of the splendid silver pieces that were found in these hoards seem to have been made in the east. Naissus (Niş) and Thessalonica (Salonica) have already been mentioned in this connection, and it appears not improbable that the Great Mildenhall Dish was created at Constantinople,[6] not long after its foundation by Constantine the Great, and shortly before it became the capital of the eastern Roman empire.

Goldsmiths and silversmiths were often freedmen or slaves,[7] and more on this subject is said in the Epilogue that follows.

EPILOGUE

There is always a lot of talk about the extent to which Roman art – and, by implication, the art of the Roman empire – is derivative: the extent, that is to say, of its derivation from, and imitation of, Greece and Etruria, a theme that has been mentioned more than once in this book. These discussions seem, quite often, to miss the point. *Every* art is, in some degree, derivative; no art is entirely, 100 per cent, original. The whole doctrine of 'originality' has a somewhat Victorian ring, and need not be reinvoked nowadays. Nevertheless, there does remain a question about Roman art, and the art of the Roman empire: is it so completely unoriginal that no such thing exists?

I hope that the present book has answered that question. The art of the Roman empire does exist, in its own right. Whatever talk there may be of origins, the art of Rome and its empire produced impressive results. I have tried to show a number of them – some of those that, as it seems to me, represent novelties and require debate and appreciation.

What needs pointing out and emphasizing, I think, even in a volume as selective as this, is the *diversity* of this art of the Roman empire. I have needed fifteen chapter headings to cover its principal manifestations, and the number could have been greatly increased. There were many different kinds of art in the Roman empire, and their essential diversity is seen in its true light when one considers them on geographical and territorial lines; when one points, that is to say, to artistic manifestations which made their appearance or reached their climax in this or that country or province outside Rome and Italy – although the central role of Rome must never be forgotten. As to the origins of the workmen concerned,

> the fact that works of art were in the main produced by slave labour and were generally in use made such [work] cheap. But even free artisans were not too well paid. In the edict of Diocletian, the daily wage of the workmen who attended to the artistic decoration of houses is based upon the supposition that they, like the rest, received their board from the landlord.
>
> The pay of the stucco-worker is the same as that of the bricklayer,

carpenter, lime-burner, carriage-maker, baker and [black]smith; that of the mosaic-worker is a sixth higher, that of the clay- and stucco-modeller half as much again, that of the portrait-painter three times as high.

The casting of statues in bronze was paid for by the pound. In the case of statues, the result of their production on a large scale was a great lowering of price.[1]

A comparatively small number of the many thousands of artists, who exercised their craft during the early centuries of the empire, are known to us by name, and nearly all of these only from their own inscriptions on their works. Notwithstanding the frequent allusions to artistic undertakings of all kinds the artists who carried them out are hardly mentioned. This is partly to be explained by the subordinate position held by artists in society, and also by the fact that artistic production was far more frequently the work of associations than of individuals, who being merely the instruments of a corporation were held, as individuals, in little regard.[2]

Yet, even so, the artists of the Roman world often produced wonderful things. One reason why this was so was the two-way process which governed artistic production in the Roman empire. What I mean by this is that Rome influenced the provinces, and the provinces influenced Rome as well[3]: when they did not do so directly, they influenced the capital through the artists from their own centres whom they dispatched, or rather allowed to migrate, to the capital.

Some of the artists and others who undertook great works of art, who possessed or hired workmen in all artistic departments, must have travelled from place to place. . . . [Yet] no doubt in the more important towns there were settlements of artists in constant employment. . . . In the second-rate towns, even, there was no lack of sculptors' workshops. . . .

[But] artists were almost always on the road. The craving for the artistic side of life throughout the whole Roman world is evidenced by the countless ruins of artistic work in every province; and the huge demand could only have been satisfied by 'colonies, expeditions, swarms of clouds of artists, and artists hovering about, ready to settle down anywhere'.[4]

That is what the art of the Roman empire is all about. Rome is always the inspirational and financial centre. But the centre would not have exercised anything like as much power if there had not been this two-way movement of art and artists between Rome and the provinces.

The two-way movement was one of the things which meant that much of the art of the empire reached a considerable standard. Not by any means all of it, of course, as I have remarked elsewhere. No art is wholly and invariably good, and obviously some of the art of the Roman empire was pretty poor, or extremely bad. But some was good, and let us not be led away by perjorative, derogatory discussion of lack of 'originality' into denying this. Because of these excellent productions this was an art which ranks high among the arts of the world. Artists today ought to be proud to have it among their forebears, and it will be useful for them to understand what it has to offer. As indeed others, too, ought to have a similar understanding, and it is in the hope of furthering such a process that this book has been written.

So who were the artists and architects of the Roman empire? As has been seen, we do not know much about them – we do know some names, but not many, relatively speaking. A few of them are Roman names, and there assuredly was a certain number of Romans engaged in these activities: those whose identities have come down to us would no doubt, being Romans, be more likely to get themselves known and named than artists and architects of other origins.

Of the latter, too, we have a few names: but only a few, such as Apollodorus of Damascus, Zeno and the Dioscurideses, of Samos and Aegeae (and cf. p. 21). May I, however, take refuge in a conjecture? I would guess that most of the great masterpieces of these successive imperial epochs were created by Greeks, or by easterners with a Greek or Greco-Roman training, who travelled to Rome and to the west, and were prompted to do so by the money which they were thus able to acquire: although what they did not manage to acquire was a sufficient reputation for their names to become known, even if very often they were the creators of masterpieces. And at least a few of the major works of the time, such as the reliefs at Tropaeum Trajani (Adamklissi), were made by local natives, of whom we know nothing.

*　　*　　*

The art of the Roman empire passed gradually into what we know as medieval art. We have seen some of the stages in this process. The huge head of Constantine the Great in the Conservatori Museum in Rome is well on the way to the hieratic portraits of Byzantium. The reliefs on the Arch of Constantine illustrate novel developments. The Basilica of Maxentius marked a sharp departure from classical basilican architecture. The massive churches of the early Christian emperors depended on the past but looked forward to future epochs. Although the mosaic-workers still laid mosaics, they began doing so on walls as well, and on the ceilings of apses. And so on. Medieval art is not the subject of this book, but it is worth while, all the same, to quote, in conclusion, this observation by E. Kjellberg and G. Säflund:

> Without any real break the art of the ancient world still lives . . . especially where ancient culture had the opportunity of establishing firm roots. There is no gulf between the art of late antiquity and that of the Middle Ages. The tasks and conditions of artists changed with the

changing state of society, but in all the wide region which had once been watered by Greek and Roman culture, both the ancient language of form and ancient ideas and symbols live on as an undying source of inspiration.[5]

LIST OF ROMAN EMPERORS

30 BC–AD 14	Augustus

The Julio-Claudians

AD 14–37	Tiberius
37–41	Gaius (Caligula)
41–54	Claudius
54–68	Nero

The civil war

68–9	Galba
69	Otho
69	Vitellius

The Flavians and their successors

69–79	Vespasian
79–81	Titus
81–96	Domitian
96–8	Nerva
98–117	Trajan
117–38	Hadrian

The Antonines: age of transition

138–61	Antoninus Pius
161–80	Marcus Aurelius
161–9	Lucius Verus
180–92	Commodus

Period of disorder

193	Pertinax
193	Didius Julianus

The Severans: the changed empire

193–211	Septimius Severus
211–17	Caracalla
211–12	Geta
[217–18	Macrinus]
218–22	Elagabalus
222–35	Severus Alexander

The military anarchy

235–8	Maximinus I 'Thrax'
238–44	Gordianus III

244–9	Philip 'the Arabian'
249–51	Trajanus Decius
251–3	Trebonianus Gallus
{ 253–9	Valerian
253–68	Gallienus

The military recovery

268–70	Claudius Gothicus
270–5	Aurelian
276–82	Probus
282–3	Carus
283–4	Carinus and Numerian

The tetrarchy

{ 284–305	Diocletian
284–305, 307–8, 310 }	Maximian
{ 305–6	Constantius I Chlorus
305–11	Galerius

Constantine the Great

306–37	Constantine I the Great
306–12	Maxentius
310–13	Maximinus II Daia
308–24	Licinius

The heirs of Constantine

337–61	Constantius II (Constantine II 337–40, Constans 337–50)
361–3	Julian the Apostate
363–4	Jovian

The divided empire

364–75	Valentinian I (in the West) (Valens in the East, 364–78)
379–95	Theodosius I (in the East; also West 394–5)
425–55	Valentinian III (in the West)
476	Fall of Western Empire to the Germans
1453	Fall of Eastern (Byzantine) Empire to the Turks

NOTES

Introduction

1 Cf. Toynbee, 1951: 55, n. 4. Strzygowski denied the supremacy of the Romans in art, stressing Asia Minor. The great eastern cities, Alexandria and Antioch, are very important in the history of Roman imperial art, cf. Hanfmann, 1975: 77; and later in this book.
2 One way of putting it is to say that the Romans 'reshaped' Hellenistic art. But on the whole subject see Boardman, 1993.
3 Friedländer, 1928: II, 311.
4 E.g. also ibid.: 303, 312 ('with the possible exception of the Celtic districts'). Friedländer stated that Rome lacked a creative power of its own. Cf. pp. 325 f.
5 But I have excluded roads and frontier walls – although a Roman might well have called their designers *artifices* (see text, below), and roads did much for social intercourse and thereby helped to create a homogeneous civilization.

    Active local élites (usually rather conservative) helped to finance local art, with strong, though rather patchy, assistance from the imperial government (of which, however, many inhabitants of the empire had little experience or conception). Indigenous languages and religions continued to survive. For the varying degrees of local influences upon art, cf. Heintze, 1990: 6. As for Rome, although it remained the central powerhouse, there was a steady decline in the export of Roman (and Italian) products from the second century AD. Class divisions at Rome also need to be considered.

6 Though Varro stressed the importance of female painters; see Friedländer, 1928: II, 327; and ibid.: 147 ff. (cf. Ch. 11, p. 9).
7 Casson, 1974: 121 f.
8 Friedländer, 1928: II, 337; because the Romans considered fine art very important, ibid.: 327; cf. 310.
9 Barrow, 1975: 97.

PART I SCULPTURE

1 Imperial portraits

1 Grant, 1982: 189, 170 and Plates.
2 Pliny the Elder, *Natural History*, XXXIV, 65 (Lysippus), XXXVI, 37 (Laocoon).
3 Grant, 1958: 26 f.
4 Kaehler, 1963: 35 f., 38. E. S. Strong, 1907–11: II, 183 f. Between 15 and 16 inches high.
5 Suetonius, *Divus Augustus*, 79.
6 Friedländer, 1928: II, 278 f., 282 f., 312.

7 Grant, 1958: 13. It was important to familiarize the army with the features of the emperor, partly in order to stress dynastic continuity. Besides, every statue and head of an emperor expresses consciousness of his mission and duties, and conveys the individual view that each of them held of himself and his position. The tendency towards realism or quasi-realism goes back to republican tradition, but there was also a tendency to make emperors and empresses younger and more handsome than they were. There were severe restrictions on the use of imperial images.

8 Toynbee, 1964: 50.

9 E.g. the sculptor Criton of Athens went to Ostia, and Zenodorus (who made the Colossus of Nero) travelled to the Arverni, Aquitania and Rome; cf. also Zeno of Aphrodisias and Novius Blaesimus. Friedländer, 1928: II, 310; cf. II, 322, I, 318, III, 16. See also Ch. 11, n. 13.

10 Zanker, 1983: 7–20; see p.7 for references to Arrian, and discussion; p.9 for the expense of transporting statues and busts from Rome; p.9, n. 83 for 'private' imperial portraits; pp. 21 ff., for busts from various provinces; p.43, n. 137, for the use and availability of local stones in the northern provinces (this was always a relevant factor everywhere else as well). There were flourishing schools of sculpture all over the empire.

11 The sculptors showed that they were well aware of the 'barbarian' origins of Maximinus I Thrax and Philip 'the Arabian'.

12 Wilkinson, 1981: 177; Heintze, 1990: 179; Pietrangeli, 1958: 126–9; Felletti Maj, 1958: 170–1, no. 193, Pl. 23, Fig. 75; Neudecker, 1988: 237–40, nn. 69 1–30.

13 We are on the way to the internal, spiritual, intangible elements in future life and art: cf. Kjellberg and Säflund, 1968: 216 ff.

14 Toynbee, 1964: 39 ff. Philip, in this bust, has been described (perhaps a little unfairly) as anxious, nervous, shifty, opportunistic, insignificant and uncertain of purpose, but crafty. Cf. Ramage and Ramage, 1991: 244.

15 Paolo Liverani, in a letter of 27 June 1994, considers it reasonable to suppose that the bust was sculpted at Rome.

16 Sydow, 1969.

17 Grant, 1993: 104 and n. 44; cf. Pl. I (p. 116).

18 For sculpture in Asia Minor under the Romans, cf. Zanker, 1983: 21–5. For non-Roman portraits of Marcus Aurelius, Grant, 1994: 144.

19 Grant, 1990: 115, n. 8.

20 Brilliant, 1974: 123.

2 Portraits of private individuals

1 Pliny the Elder, *Natural History*, XXXV, ii, 10.

2 Friedländer, 1928: II, 296.

3 Grant, 1960: 277. 'Terracotta, stone and marble portraits of the next few generations have facial structures suggesting that they are copies of reminiscences of death-masks, since they stress prominent bones and cartilages rather than the surface irregularities which were smoothed out by death; and the frequency with which old men and women are represented may be prompted not only by the desire to sum up a biography but by the existence of such masks.' cf. pp. 276–9. On the other hand, as stated in the text, the mummy-heads in Egypt do not mostly show old people.

4 Mansuelli, 1963: 174, Pl. 53.

5 Lucian, for example, found education (*paideia*) more attractive than the dirty art of sculpture; Grant, 1994: 107.

6 *Pace* Friedländer, 1928: II, 296.

7 *Mémoires présentés par divers savants à l'Académie des Inscriptions et Belles Lettres*, 1er sér., XI (1901): 329–44.

8 La Baume, n.d. 43–50.

9 Toynbee, 1964: 56–63.

10 Cf. also Aphrodisias, described above.

11 On Roman wealth from the east cf. Cottrell, 1960: 133.

12 In many ways the Palmyrenes succeeded the Nabataeans.

13 A Ny Carlsberg Glyptotek example is illustrated here. Another such woman was Arminia; see Richmond, 1963: 34, Pl. II(1). And another was Agmat, daughter of Hagago; see Grant, 1968: Pl. 4.

14 Fedden, 1946: 147.

15 Richmond, 1963: 53f., cf. 43.

16 Stoneman, 1992: 69 f.

17 Richmond, 1963: Pl. II(2).

3 Imperial reliefs

1 A processional way, between three-storeyed walls, led to the temple.

2 Grant, 1990: 113 ff.

3 Walters, 1911: 52 (reconstruction); Ramage and Ramage, 1991: 163; Richmond, 1965: 307. For arguments about the date, Florescu, 1963: 56 f. The town of Tropaeum Trajani grew up in the valley below; most of its remains are of the time of Constantine.

4 The artists of the Tropaeum Trajani liked flat patterns and presented a sponge-like surface full of holes made by drilling, employing a technique that had originally perhaps been used for wood.

5 Cf. the Jupiter column at Moguntiacum (Mainz), carved by Gaulish sculptors (Samus and Severus). Even the Ara Pacis reliefs at Rome had been inspired by Hellenistic Pergamum (Bergama); many marble masons, travelling westwards from Greece and Asia Minor, undertook reliefs.

6 On some of the later history of imperial reliefs, cf. Grant, 1993: 103 f. (Arch of Constantine). Reliefs of a non-imperial character also deserve some mention: e.g. silver (Ch. 15) and *terra sigillata* (Medri, 1992).

4 Sarcophagi

1 There had been isolated examples earlier.

2 Marble from Proconnesus island (Marmara Adasi) was used.

3 E.g. the famous Ludovisi sarcophagus (*c.* AD 250), in the Museo delle Terme at Rome.

4 E.g. the Aspendus sarcophagus; see Vermeule, 1968: 61.

5 Christian sarcophagi often showed scenes from the Old Testament as prefigurations of the New Testament.

6 Brilliant, 1974: 102 f., 109, Fig. II, 21a and b; height 4 feet 9 inches. Ramage and Ramage, 1991: 216, Fig. 8.32. The sarcophagus has been dated to the third quarter of the second century AD.

7 It has been suggested that it may have been an Italian imitation of an Asian import; Toynbee, 1965: 105. On a tomb from Andematunnum (Langres) it is recorded that the dead man insisted on the use of marble from Luna (Luni) in Italy; T. F. C. Blagg, 'Society and the artist', in Wacher, 1987: II, 725.

PART II ARCHITECTURE

Introduction: Architecture as an art

1 Quoting from Semper's *Der Stil* (I, 479).
2 Friedländer, 1928: II, 324.
3 Vitruvius I, 1, 3; cf. Friedländer, 1928: II, 596, n. 249, on the relatively superior status of architects. For Vitruvius cf. Pollitt, 1966: 120 ff.
4 Friedländer, 1928: II, 324 f., contested this, arguing that most of the empire's principal architects were Romans.
5 Le Corbusier, 1928.
6 Pevsner, 1943: I; cf. also Crimson and Lubbock, 1994.
7 Cf. Rossi, 1971: 19, 28, 32, 121, 174, 183. Apollodorus also designed Trajan's Arch at Ancona. Later, however, he incurred the disfavour of Hadrian and returned to Damascus.

5 Pagan temples

1 Reconstruction in Brilliant, 1974: 42 f. (Schulz); Abbate, 1972: 88, Fig. 56; Boethius (ed. Ward-Perkins), 1970: 570, Fig. 814 (Wiegand). Grant, 1994: 134. A major architectural triumph was the Temple of Zeus (Jupiter) Heliopolitanus at Heliopolis (Baalbek) in Syria. This displays the Syrian adoption, with variations, of the Italian formula of combining temple with extensive precinct. Its date has been disputed. Probably John Malalas's attribution of the temple to Antoninus Pius was wrong. Its construction may have been begun in the first century AD, although the completion of the project may well be dated to Antoninus Pius, who was known to have helped cities, at a time when construction or reconstruction could be adjusted to the more sophisticated tastes of the second century.
2 Wheeler, 1964: 20. The columns of the principal temple at Heliopolis are 65 feet high and 7 feet in diameter. A block of hewn stone in a quarry nearby is 60 feet long and weighs 1,500 tons. These huge pieces of masonry seem closer to Egypt than to Greece. Probably the Emperor Philip (AD 244–9), an Arabian from not very far away, did a good deal to enrich Heliopolis. The adjacent 'Temple of Bacchus' was very lavishly decorated; Grant, 1994: 134, Fig. 24.

6 Houses

1 Hanfmann, 1975: 17.
2 Grant, 1960: 260 f.
3 Grant, 1971a: 113 f., 117, 121, 124. Rich house-owners went outside Italy for their tastes and materials; thus Julius Caesar's chief engineer Mamurra obtained some of the marble for his house from Euboea (some also came from Etruria).
4 Grant, 1971a; 112 f.
5 Boethius (ed. Ward-Perkins), 1970: Fig. 111; McKay, 1975: 89 ff. and Fig. 28 (reconstruction); Grant, 1960: 308, Fig. xxiii (Gismondi).
6 Ostian houses had three or four floors. Their maximum permitted height was $65\frac{1}{2}$ feet. They were made of red or yellow brick. There were four different types of apartment, three types of façade, and three types of balcony.
7 Grant, 1971b: 132 f. Pro-Roman monarchs *inside* the empire also possessed imposing palaces, notably that ascribed to Tiberius Claudius Cogidubnus at Fishbourne in Britain.
8 Adam Smith, 1966.
9 Cf. Yadin, 1966: 15 f., 205 f., etc.
10 McKay, 1975: 215 f.

11 R. J. A. Wilson, 1983: 85; Carandini, Ricci and De Vos, 1982. Abbate, 1972: 94, comments on the singular combination of tradition and innovation in this sort of late Roman architecture.

12 There are forty-two polychrome pavements, covering 3,500 square yards. Originally, there were also marble plaques, frescoes and statues.

13 Brown 1961: Pls 92, 93; Boethius (ed. Ward-Perkins), 1970: Figs 200, 201; Wilkes, 1993; Andreae, 1978: 555 ff. (Neumann); Kaehler, 1963: 202, 316–21.

14 Grant, 1968: 106.

15 Frontier fortifications had more or less collapsed. But the military analogies of Diocletian's palace, with its four groups of buildings, are disputed (cf. McNally, 1994: 180), although its owner perhaps expected hostile attempts on his life (if we assume that he had a hand in the design). In any case, it can be said that Diocletian, in retirement, was consciously withdrawing from an increasingly alien world, and that this is what his palace reflects. Attached to the mansion was his mausoleum, reached by a monumental approach. We must think of centralized buildings such as this mausoleum (and Hadrian's much earlier Pantheon) when we come to Christian architecture. And indeed, in the whole complex, we can see Roman styles gradually moving towards Romanesque (Wheeler, 1964: 14).

7 Places of entertainment

1 Andreae, 1978: 56 f., 805 (Wilson's reconstruction); Robertson, 1969: 29 ff.; Ramage and Ramage, 1991: 105, Fig. 727; Grant, 1994: 133, Fig. 26. The interior is partly conjectural. The son of Tiberius Julius Celsus Polemaeanus was Tiberius Julius Aquila Polemaeanus (consul AD 110).

2 Brown, 1961: 30 f.

3 Keay, 1988: 124 f., 138.

4 Broughton, 1929: 6.

5 Croutier, 1992: 81, 83, 85 f.

6 For a list of Roman spas cf. Casson, 1974: 134, 142, 345. Some denounced the luxury of these amenities. But hydrotherapy was taken seriously.

7 Aquae Sulis, the town, covered only 22 acres. Later, it was surrounded by a defensive wall. Cf. Branigan and Fowler (1995). Another fine set of baths was at Viroconium (Wroxeter in Shropshire).

8 Croutier, 1992: 116 ff., 123.

9 Robertson, 1969: 276 f. and figs, reconstruction in Leacroft and Leacroft, 1969: 29. On this region cf. Friedländer, 1928: II, 243: 'The massive and well-preserved ruins in Pamphylia and Pisidia . . . afford the best idea of the number, splendour and greatness of the cities of Asia Minor at this time.'

10 A frequent difference between Greek and Roman theatres is that the former are often cut out of rock, whereas the latter are not, and stand independently.

11 Pliny the Elder, *Natural History*, XXXVI, xxiv, 119.

12 Cf. Wells, 1984: 248, 254; Wilkinson, 1981: 163.

13 King, 1982: 109. An amphitheatre was also called *arena*, because it was filled with that material (sand). Wooden construction was unsafe, cf. Tacitus, *Annals*, IV, 62–3 on Fidenae (Castel Giubileo). The early amphitheatres of northern Italy and Gaul were made of timber.

14 But the oldest amphitheatre known is at Pompeii. Amphitheatres were fairly rare, but not non-existent, in the east; Herodes Atticus built one at Athens.

15 *Blue Guide*, p. 778. But is the Nemausus amphitheatre Augustan, or a later copy of the Colosseum? (Or both: the latter a subsequent stage?) There were thirty-five tiers of seats for 24,000 spectators. Five radial tunnels facilitated entrance and exit. Seats were reserved for the town dignitaries and for boatmen of the Rivers Rhodanus (Rhône)

and Arar (Saône). Shows were also given, throughout the empire, in circuses or stadia.

16 Perhaps the slightly larger amphitheatre at Arelate (Arles) is a decade or two later; Krautheimer, 1965: 353. The amphitheatres at Arelate and Nemausus are the best preserved in Gaul. Cf. also Bromwich, 1993.

17 James, 1884: 171 f.

18 MacKendrick, 1962: 476 f. The stadium (rebuilt in 1896) lay in a hollow between two hills. The River Ilissus flowed by until recently. See also Walker and Cameron, 1989. For the Odeon of Herodes Atticus, see Grant, 1994: Fig. 25.

8 Arches, bridges, aqueducts

1 Boethius (ed. Ward-Perkins), 1970: 482. To what extent these triumphal arches were derived from Greek or Etruscan sources has been much disputed. At any rate, with the help of concrete, they were acclimatized at Rome by the end of the first century BC, and covered with rich decorations.

2 An outstandingly fine arch was that of Lepcis Magna (recently restored); Raven, 1993: 118, 158. The Arch of Caracalla at Theveste (Tebessa) is also notable.

3 Travellers from Lambaesis (Tazzoult) arrived by this road. Grooves for wheeled traffic are still visible beneath the Arch.

4 MacKendrick, 1969: 163 f. There were also many other Roman bridges in Spain. Cf. now O'Connor, 1994.

5 Keay, 1988: 137 f.

6 There were four such aqueducts at Lugdunum (Lyon) in Gaul. As for Rome, 165 million gallons of water flowed into the city every day, through thirteen aqueducts.

7 An alternative dating places the aqueduct in the first quarter of the second century AD. See Wheeler, 1964: 151, Fig. 134; Leacroft and Leacroft, 1969: 23 (reconstruction).

8 Frontinus, *De Aquis Urbis Romae*, I, 16.

9 Grant, 1960: 273; Croutier, 1992: 83.

10 Brown, 1961: 30 f.

9 Pagan basilicas

1 Boethius (ed. Ward-Perkins), 1970: 581 ff. The roofs of basilicas were habitually flat, and supported by timber trusses.

2 ibid.: 477, Fig. 179 (reconstruction of interior), p. 1247. A shallow clerestory is assumed. The central feature and some of the decorations on the north-eastern façade seem to have been afterthoughts (of a relatively early date).

3 E.g. the distinctive masonry formula of the outer wall; cf. D. E. Strong, 1961: 62.

4 Wheeler, 1964: 16, 20, 22.

5 Grant, 1970: 153 ff.; cf. Hanfmann, 1975: 74, no. 32; Wheeler, 1964: 115 (reconstruction); Robertson, 1969: 2614 (reconstruction).

6 E. S. Strong, 1929: I, 172 f.

7 Hanfmann, 1975. The huge half-circular windows, one for each bay, together with the arches and vaults, present a conscious rhythmical effect. Brick-faced concrete is the main material, and there was a stucco covering, imitating masonry. With its three massive cross-vaults rising to 114 feet, and an overall length of 240 feet and width of 75 feet, this was the largest hall in the ancient world (larger than the nave and choir of Westminster Abbey and more than three times as wide), overshadowing the puny individual and making a political statement asserting the primacy of Rome: it was the last great official building in the city. The vaults of the Basilica of Maxentius made it very different from its forerunners; it was like a bath, but isolated and longer.

8 Grant, 1993: Roman concrete, from which all air had been expelled, was only improved on in the nineteenth century, by Portland cement.

10 Christian architecture

1 Grant, 1993: 191 f.
2 ibid.
3 Though Constantine's encouragement of the arts promoted a certain growth in skills.
4 Grant, 1993: 191 f.
5 But mention should also be made of Constantine's building of the Lateran and Santa Croce churches in Rome.
6 Though the original apse of Sixtus III was not separated from the triumphal arch of the church, as now.
7 Originally a pagan basilica had stood on the site (at the summit of the Cispian Hill). The mosaics of S. Maria Maggiore suggest a close link with North Africa. Krautheimer, 1965.
8 ibid.: 78 f., Pl. XVII.
9 Pereira, 1968: 67 f.
10 Grant, 1993: 197 f.
11 A. Wear, *Times Literary Supplement*, 1 March 1994, p. 27.
12 Pagan forerunners included the Pantheon.
13 Krautheimer, 1965: 30, 32.
14 ibid.: 35 f., 50, Pl. 11A.
15 Gibson and Taylor, 1994: 73 f., 84.

PART III OTHER ARTS

11 Paintings, Stucco, Textiles

1 Painting ranked quite high as a liberal art, Abbate, 1972: 23. Pliny the Elder, *Natural History*, XXXV, devoted a lot of space to the subject. There were also some easel paintings (cf. text).
2 Rozenburg, 1994: 9.
3 Grant, 1971a: 141 f., 166; Rozenberg, 1994: 12 f., 162, n. 11. Originals are usually untraceable. The copies are sometimes flashy rather than faithful. Black, yellow and red dominated: lampblack (made of soot) and yellow earth were obtainable.
4 McKay, 1975: 145, 151, 153 ff.
5 Wheeler, 1964: 199, Fig. 184, cf. 197 (Naples 9418, A. Maiuri, *Mus. Naz. Napoli*, Pl. xviii).
6 For the 'Four' Styles, see Grant, 1971a: 142, 149, 152, 155; Rozenberg, 1994: 11 f., 162, nn. 6–9.
7 It was said that a certain Ludius (or Studius), in the time of Augustus, invented bucolic landscapes. But a much earlier date, in the third century BC, is also suggested. There was a sentimental interest in country landscapes in contemporary literature. Self-conscious romanticism is not lacking; see Friedländer, 1928: I, 138 ff. (Appendix XXII).
8 Grant, 1971a: 167; cf. Hanfmann, 1975: 278, Pl. xxxii.
9 For the encaustic technique, see Pliny the Elder, *Natural History*, XXXV, 122. Early painted 'portraits' had also occurred elsewhere, e.g. at Stabiae in Campania: and there a later round painting of Septimius Severus and Julia Domna and Caracalla; Toynbee, 1965: Fig. 74. For the interesting prominence of female portraits ('Aline' is famous), see Introduction, n. 6 and Fig. 3, etc.

10 Hanfmann, 1975: 304. Others came from Antinoupolis (Antinoe, Hadrianopolis: Sheikh-Ibada), where Antinous was drowned; cf. n. 12.

11 ibid. On the interaction between Greco-Roman and Egyptian traditions see also Friedländer, 1928: II, 304.

12 Zaloscer, 1961: Pl. 24; Thompson, 1976: Pl. 17 (from Antinoupolis).

13 Some painters travelled widely; e.g. Annaeus Atticus, who was buried at Ostia, came from Aquitania. See also Ch. 1, n. 10.

14 Rozenberg, 1994: 9, 147, 153.

15 Vitruvius, VII, 3.5; Pliny the Elder, op. cit., XXXVI, 176 f; cf. Grant, 1994: 144 f.

16 Wheeler, 1964: 214 and Figs 196, 197, 214, 215.

17 Grant 1971a: 186. Other forms of enterprise that perhaps deserve classification as 'art' are Roman glass (see Harden, 1987), and *terra sigillata* (see Bémont and Jacob, 1986).

12 Mosaics

1 Grant, 1971a: 172.

2 Mosaics from Thuburbo Majus (Henchir el Kasbat), Hadrumetum (Sousse), Bulla Regia (Hammam Daradji) and Thysdrus (El Djem), besides Carthage, are especially notable.

3 Rostovtzeff, 1960: Pl. xviii(1). It is unusual to blend the theme of the Seasons with pictures of a house and its activities.

4 Raven, 1993: 164 f.

5 Dunbabin, 1978: 252, no. 39, Pl. 109, 119 ff.

6 Fischer, 1971: 9, 7.

7 The Greek mosaicist Publius Aelius Harpocration (Proclus) settled at Perinthus (Marmaraereğlisi, Ereğli) in Thrace (see Toynbee, 1964: 230) and travelled widely (see Friedländer, 1928: II, 310). A mosaic from Juliobona (Lillebonne) in Gaul, now at Rouen, was made by Titus Sennius Felix from Puteoli (Pozzuoli) and a pupil from Carthage(?). Mosaicists in North Africa could obtain chippings for their *tesserae* from imported Greek marbles; Toynbee, op. cit.: 229.

13 Coins and medallions

1 A. Pope, quoted by Quennell, 1971: 34.

2 Grant, 1958: 13 f.; Bastien, 1994: I–III.

3 Grant, 1958: 14 ff.; cf. Grant, 1960: 66 f., 283.

4 Grant, 1958: 54; cf. Mattingly and Sydenham, 1930: III, 331 ff. It is hardly surprising, then, that Hadrian was not popular with the senatorial class at Rome; the medallions of his successor Antoninus Pius were, in part, an attempt to redress the balance. For, under Hadrian, Hellenism had become a dominant movement. But even as early as Augustus, attempts had been made to endow each province with a kind of corporate existence.

5 Sutherland, 1955: 15 f.

6 To which should be added the 'provincial' issues (which were also official).

7 Grant, 1958: 73 ff.

8 Grant, 1946: 477 ff.

9 Vermeule, 1986: III, 5, 9, 15, 25, 33 f., 34, 41, 62, 81, 83, 93.

10 Grant, 1994: 146.

11 Grant, 1954: 98.

12 Toynbee, 1986: 193 ff. The medallions portrayed Hercules and Cacus, Aeneas and Ascanius, Navius Attus, Horatius Cocles, Aesculapius, and the Pinarii and Potitii.

13 Vermeule, 1986: III, *passim*; and plates.

14 Gems and jewels

1 Walters, 1911: 118 f. Mention should be made of the Portland Vase (British Museum), a blown dark blue and opaque white amphora with cameo-cut scenes in relief, probably showing the marriage of Peleus and Thetis; Henig, 1983: 217 and Fig. 181. For gem-cutters see Furtwängler, 1900: II, 232–46.

2 Brilliant, 1993: 116, Fig. II.35.

3 Hellenistic jewellery had introduced innovative new forms and new motifs and systems invented by decorators (*diatretarii*).

4 Suetonius, *Augustus*, 50; cf. Pollitt, 1966: 117.

5 For the caravan city of Mampsis see Rosenthal, 1973: 80, 87.

6 Syrian finds of jewellery, in particular, continued prominently.

15 Silver

1 Kent and Painter, 1977: 15–19. For a list of hoards, see Toynbee, 1964: 160, cf. 87a, b. The origins of the 'Sevso' hoard (Lebanon, Hungary, ex-Yugoslavia?) remain disputed. There is now the Hoxne hoard; see Bland and Johns, 1994: 25. For ancient gold, see Williams and Ogden, 1994; and Pirzio Biroli Stefanelli, 1991; and an exhibition was staged in the British Museum in 1994. Cf. a find near Devizes.

2 Kent and Painter, 1977: 33.

3 ibid.: no. 54.

4 Olympias, the mother of Alexander III the Great, is portrayed on a silver bowl, and so perhaps is Alexander himself.

5 Kent and Painter, 1977: 33.

6 But a portrait of Licinius on a bowl in the 'Munich Treasure' (origin disputed; cf. 'Sevso' hoard, n. 1) resembles that on coins issued at Heraclea (Perinthus). One must bear in mind the possibility of silverware being made at centres other than Constantinople, such as Carthage; and Rome, Alexandria and Antioch, as well as Constantinople, are personified by statuettes in the Esquiline Treasure. The contents of the Mildenhall Treasure were not made in Britain; Toynbee, 1964: 137, against T. C. Lethbridge, *The Times*, 11 July 1946.

7 One of them, Marcus Canuleius Zosimus, is praised (*Inscriptiones Latinae Selectae* 7645).

Epilogue

1 Friedländer, 1928: II, 319.

2 ibid.: 325.

3 For the increased role and power of the provinces, see Grant, 1994: 161 f.

4 Friedländer, 1928: II, 310; I, 318. The quotation is from Goethe. Travelling in the Roman empire, Friedländer suggested, was more extensive than in Europe up to the nineteenth century.

5 Kjellberg and Säflund, 1968: 219.

SELECT BIBLIOGRAPHY

I ANCIENT WRITINGS

1 Greek

Arrian of Bithynia (north-west Asia Minor), second century AD. Governor of Cappadocia; writer of military treatises, historian and preserver of Epictetus.
Lucian of Samosata, born *c.* AD 120. Satirist, philosopher, writer on many subjects.
Pollux of Naucratis, second century AD. Scholar and rhetorician.
Polybius of Megalopolis, *c.* 200–after 118 BC. Historian.

2 Latin

Cicero of Arpinum, 106–43 BC. Orator, writer on oratory and philosophy, letter-writer, statesman.
Frontinus, *c.* AD 30–104. Out of many works (e.g. on land-surveying and military science and strategy), a two-volume account of the water supply of Rome (*De Aquis Urbis Romae*) has survived.
Pliny the Elder of Comum, AD 23/4–79. Officer, administrator, historian, scientist.
Suetonius of Hippo Regius, *c.* AD 69–after 121/2. Biographer.
Tacitus, *c.* AD 55–120. Roman historian; consul. Son-in-law of Agricola.
Vitruvius, first century BC. Architect, military engineer, writer on architecture (*De Architectura*).

II MODERN WRITINGS

Abbate, F. (ed.) (1972) *Roman Art*, London: Octopus.
Adam Smith, G. (1966 [1894]) *The Historical Geography of the Holy Land*, London.
Akten der Wissenschaft: Konferenz Römische Porträt, Berlin: Humboldt University, 1983.
Andreae, B. (1963) *Studien zur römischen Grabkunst*, Heidelberg.
Andreae, B. (1978) *The Art of Rome*, London: Macmillan.
Andreae, B. and Kyreleis, H. (eds) (1975) *Neue Forschungen in Pompeji usw.*, Recklinghausen.
Andrews, I. (1978) *Pompeii*, Cambridge/London: Cambridge University Press.
Auguet, R. (1994) *Cruelty and Civilization: The Roman Games*, reprint, London: Routledge.
Augusti, S. (1957) *La technique de la peinture pompeienne*, Naples.
Augusti, S. (1967) *I colori pompeiani*, Rome.
Barbet, A. (ed.) (1983) *La peinture murale romaine dans les provinces de l'Empire*, Oxford/London: Oxford University Press (1982 conference).

Barbet, A. (1985) *La peinture murale romaine*, Paris.

Barrow, R. H. (1975) *The Romans*, New York: Viking Penguin.

Bastien, P. (1994) *Le buste monétaire des empereans romains*, Vols I–III, Paris.

Becatti, G. (1978 [1965, 1971]) *L'arte dell'eta classica* (Storia dell'arte classica e italiana 1), Florence.

Bémont, C. and Jacob, S.-P. (eds) (1986) *La terre sigillée gallo-romaine* (Documents d'archéologie française), Paris: Maison des Sciences de L'Homme.

Berciu, D. (1978) *Daco-Romania*, Geneva: Nagel.

Bergmann, M. (1977) *Studien zum Römischen Porträt des dritten Jahrhunderts nach Christus*, Bonn.

Bertman, S. (1975) *Art and the Romans*, Lawrence, KS: Coronado Press.

Beyen, H. C. (1938) *Die Pompejanische Wanddekoration*, The Hague: Nijhoff.

Bianchi Bandinelli, R. (1969) *L'arte romana al centro di potere*, Milan.

Bianchi Bandinelli, R. and Becatti, G. (1968) *Pittura e pittori nell'antichità*, Rome.

Bianchi Bandinelli, R. and Paribeni, E. (1993 [1976]) *Grecia: L'arte dell'antichità classica*, Rome.

Bianchi Bandinelli, R. and Torelli, M. (1986 [1976]) *Etruria-Roma: L'arte dell'antichità classica*, reprint, Rome.

Blanckenhagen, P. H. von (1949/50) *Das Bild des Menschen in der römischen Kunst*, Marburg.

Bland, R. and Johns, C. (1994) *The Hoxne Treasure*, London: British Museum

Boardman, J. (ed.) (1993) *Oxford Illustrated History of Classical Art*, Oxford/London: Oxford University Press.

Boardman, J. (1995) *The Diffusion of Classical Art in Antiquity*, London: Thames & Hudson.

Boethius, A. (1970) *Etruscan and Roman Architecture*, ed. J. B. Ward-Perkins, Harmondsworth, Mx: Penguin.

Borda, M. (1958) *La pittura romana*, Milan: Società Editrice Libraria.

Brailsford, J. W. (1955) *The Mildenhall Treasure*, 2nd edn, London: British Museum.

Branigan, K. and Fowler, P. J. (eds) (1995) *The Roman West Country*, forthcoming.

Breckenridge, J. D. (1968) *Likeness: A Conceptual History of Ancient Portraiture*, Evanston, IL: Northwestern University Press.

Brilliant, R. (1974) *Roman Art*, Oxford: Phaidon.

Brilliant, R. (1993) *Commentary on Roman Art: Selected Studies*, London: Pindar Press.

Brion, M. (1960) *Pompeii and Herculaneum*, London: Elek.

Bromwich, J. (1993) *The Roman Remains of Southern France*, London: Routledge.

Broughton, T. R. S. (1929) *The Romanization of Africa Proconsularis*, Baltimore, MD: Johns Hopkins University Press; reprinted (1968) New York: AMS Press.

Brown, F. E. (1961) *Roman Architecture*, London: George Braziller/ Prentice-Hall.

Browning, I. (1979) *Palmyra*, London: Chatto & Windus; Toronto: Clarke, Irwin.

Burn, L. (1991) *The British Museum Book of Greek and Roman Art*, London: British Museum.

Burnett, A. (1991) *Coins*, London: British Museum.

Burnett, A. Amandry, M. and Ripollès P. P. (1992) *Roman Provincial Coinage*, Vol. I, London: British Museum; Paris: Bibliothèque Nationale.

Calderini, A. (1930) *Aquileia Romana* (Studia Historica 81), Rome; reprinted 1972.

Calza G., Calza, R. and Becatti, G. (1981) *Ostia*, 12th edn, Rome: Istituto Poligrafico dello Stato.

Calza, G. and Nash, E. (1959) *Ostia*, Florence: Sansoni.

Carandini, A., Ricci, A. and De Vos, M. (1982) *Filosofiana: La villa di Piazza Armerina*, 2 vols, Palermo: Flaccovio.

Carson, R. A. G. (1990) *Coins of the Roman Empire*, London: Routledge.

Casson, L. (1974) *Travel in the Ancient World*, London: Allen & Unwin.

Cerulli Irelli, G. *et al.* (1990) *Pompejanische Wandmalerei*, Stuttgart/Zurich: Belser.

Chevalier, R. (1986) *Ostie antique: ville et port*, Paris.

Clarke, J. R. (1994) *The Houses of Roman Italy 100 BC–AD 250: Ritual, Space and Decoration*, Berkeley/Los Angeles, CA: University of California Press.

Coche de la Ferté, E. (1962) *Antique Jewellery*, Berne: Hallway.

Cornell, T. and Matthews, J. (1982) *Atlas of the Roman World*, Oxford: Phaidon.

Cottrell, L. (1960) *Wonders of Antiquity*, London: Longman; 1963 London: Pan Books.

Crema, L. (1967) *Manuale di storia dell'architettura antica*, 2nd edn, Milan.

Crimson, M. and Lubbock, J. (1994) *Architecture: Art or Profession?* Manchester: Manchester University Press.

Croutier, A. (1992) *Taking the Waters*, New York: Abbeville Press.

Cumont, F. (1942) *Recherches sur le symbolisme funéraire des Romains* (Bibliothèque de l'archéologie et de l'histoire), Paris.

Curl, J. S. (1992) *Classical Architecture*, London: Batsford.

Curtius, L. (1929) *Die Wandmalerei Pompejis*, Leipzig: Seeman; reprinted (1960) Hildesheim: Olms.

Dawson, C. M. (1944) *Romano-Campanian Mythological Landscape Painting*, New Haven, CT: Yale University Press.

Delbrueck, R. M. (1912) *Antike Porträts*, Bonn: Marcus & Weber.

Demargne, P. (ed.) (1965) *Le rayonnement des civilisations grecque et romaine sur les cultures périphériques*, Paris: De Boccard.

De Vos, A. and De Vos, M. (1982) *Pompei, Ercolano, Stabia*, Rome: Laterza.

Die Bildnisse des Augustus: Herrscherbild und Politik in Kaiserlichen Rom (exhibition), Munich, 1979.

Dunbabin, K. M. D. (1978) *The Mosaics of Roman North Africa*, Oxford/London: Oxford University Press.

Duruy, V. (1972) *The World of the Romans*, Geneva: Minerva.

Fedden, R. (1946) *Syria*, London: Robert Hale.

Felletti Maj, B. M. (1958) *Iconografia romana imperiale da Severo Alessandro a Marco Aurelio Carino*, Rome.

Ferrero, D. de B. (1974) *Teatri classici in Asia Minore*, Rome: L'Erma.

Finley, M. I. (1977) *Atlas of Classical Archaeology*, London: Chatto & Windus.

Fischer, P. (1971) *Mosaic: History and Technique*, London: Thames & Hudson.

Florescu, P. B. (1965) *Tropaeum Trajani: Das Siegesdenkmal von Adamklissi*, Bucharest/Bonn.

Franke, P. R. and Hirmer, M. (1961) *Römische Kaiserporträts im Münzbild*, Munich: Hirmer.

Friedländer, L. (1928) *Roman Life and Manners in the Early Empire*, 2nd edn, London: Routledge (translation of 7th edn of *Sittengeschichte Roms*).

Frova, A. (1961) *L'arte di Roma e del mondo romano*, Turin: Unione Tipografica.

Furtwängler, A. (1900) *Die Antiken Gemmen*, Leipzig.

Gage, J. (1993) *Colour and Culture: Practice and Meaning from Antiquity to Abstraction*, London: Thames & Hudson.

Garcia ý Bellido, A. (1979) *Arte romana*, 2nd edn, Madrid.

Gazda, E. K. (ed.) (1977) *Roman Portraiture: Ancient and Modern Revivals*, Ann Arbor, MI: University of Michigan Press.

Gazda, E. K. (ed.) (1991) *Roman Art in the Private Sphere*, Ann Arbor, MI: University of Michigan Press.

Giardina, A. (ed.) (1993) *The Romans*, Chicago: Chicago University Press.

Gibson, S. and Taylor, J. (1994) *Beneath the Church of the Holy Sepulchre; Jerusalem: The Archaeology and Early History of Traditional Golgotha* (Palestine Exploration Fund), London.

Goldscheider, L. (1940) *Roman Portraits*, London: Allen & Unwin.

Grant, M. (1946) *From Imperium to Auctoritas*, Cambridge/London: Cambridge University Press; reprinted 1969, 1978.

Grant, M. (1954) *Roman Imperial Money*, London: Nelson; reprinted 1972.

Grant, M. (1958) *Roman History from Coins*, Cambridge/London: Cambridge University Press; reprinted 1968.

Grant, M. (1960) *The World of Rome*, London: Weidenfeld & Nicolson; reprinted 1974, 1987.

Grant, M. (1968) *The Climax of Rome*, London: Weidenfeld & Nicolson; reprinted 1990.

Grant, M. (1970) *The Roman Forum*, London: Weidenfeld & Nicolson.

Grant, M. (1971a) *Cities of Vesuvius*, London: Weidenfeld & Nicolson; reprinted 1976.

Grant, M. (1971b) *Herod the Great*, London: Weidenfeld & Nicolson.

Grant, M. (1980) *The Etruscans*, London: Weidenfeld & Nicolson.

Grant, M. (1981) *The Dawn of the Middle Ages*, New York: McGraw-Hill.

Grant, M. (1982) *From Alexander to Cleopatra* (*the Hellenistic Greeks*), London: Weidenfeld & Nicolson.

Grant, M. (1990) *The Visible Past*, London: Weidenfeld & Nicolson.

Grant, M. (1993) *The Emperor Constantine*, London: Weidenfeld & Nicolson.

Grant, M. (1994) *The Antonines: Age of Transition*, London: Routledge.

Grant, M. and Kitzinger, R. (1988) *Civilization of the Ancient Mediterranean: Greece and Rome*, 3 vols, New York: Scribner.

Gruen, E. S. (1989) *Studies in Greek Culture and Roman Policy* (Cincinnati Classical Studies VIII), Amsterdam: Brill.

Gruen, E. S. (1992) *Culture and National Identity in Republican Rome*, Ithaca, NY: Cornell University Press.

Hafner, G. (1969) *The Art of Rome, Etruria and Magna Graecia*, New York: Harry Abrams.

Hamberg, P. G. (1945) *Studies in Roman Imperial Art*, Copenhagen: Munksgaard.

Hanfmann, G. M. A. (1953) *Observations on Roman Portraiture*, Brussels: Latomus.

Hanfmann, G. M. A. (1975) *Roman Art*, New York: Norton.

Hannestad, N. (1986) *Roman Art and Imperial Policy*, Aarhus: Jutland Archaeological Society.

Harden, D. (1987) *Glass of the Caesars*, London: British Museum Press/Oxbow Press.

Harl, K. (1987) *Civic Coins and Greek Politics in the Roman East AD 180–275*, Berkeley, CA: University of California Press.

Heintze, H. von (1961) *Römische Porträtplastik aus sieben Jahrhunderten*, Stuttgart: Günther.

Heintze, H. von (1990 [1972] *Roman Art: The Herbert History of Art and Architecture*, London: Herbert Press.

Hekler, A. (1912) *Greek and Roman Portraits*, London: Heinemann.

Henig, M. (ed.) (1983) *A Handbook of Roman Art*, London: Phaidon; reprinted 1992.

Henig, M. (ed.) (1990) *Architecture and Architectural Sculpture in the Roman Empire*, Oxford: Committee for Archaeology, University of Oxford.

Henig, M. and King, A. (eds) (1986) *Pagan Gods and Shrines in the Roman Empire*, Oxford/London: Oxford University Press.

Higgins, R. A. (1961) *Greek and Roman Jewellery*, London: Methuen.

Higgins, R. A. (1965) *Jewellery from Classical Lands*, London: British Museum.

Hinks, R. P. (1935) *Greek and Roman Portrait Sculpture*, London: British Museum.

Ippel, A. (1927) *Römische Porträts*, Bielefeld/Leipzig: Velhagen & Klasing.

James, H. (1884) *A Little Tour in France*, Boston, MA: J. R. Osgood & Co.

Jenkyns, R. (ed.) (1993) *The Legacy of Rome*, 2nd edn, Oxford/London: Oxford University Press.

Jewellery through 7000 Years, London: British Museum, 1976.

Jücker, H. (1950) 'Vom Verhältnis der Römer zur bildenden Kunst der Griechen', Bamberg: dissertation, University of Zurich.

Kaehler, H. (1963) *Rome and her Empire*, London: Methuen.

Kahane, P. P. (1969) *Ancient and Classical Art*, London: Thames & Hudson.

Kaschnitz-Weinberg, G. von (1962–3) *Römische Kunst*, Reinbeck: Rowohlt.

Kaschnitz-Weinberg, G. von (1965) *Römische Bildnisse*, Berlin: Mann.

Keay, S. J. (1988) *Roman Spain*, Berkeley, CA: University of California Press.

Kent, J. P. C. and Painter, K. S. (1977) *Wealth of the Roman World AD 300–700*, London: British Museum.

Kent, J. P. C., Hirmer, M. and Hirmer, A. (1978) *Roman Coins*, London: Thames & Hudson.

King, A. (1982) *Archaeology of the Roman Empire*, London: Hamlyn

Kjellberg, E. and Säflund, G. (1968) *Greek and Roman Art: 3000 BC to AD 500*, London: Faber & Faber.

Kleiner, D. E. E. (1993) *Roman Sculpture*, New Haven, CT: Yale University Press.

Koch, H. (1949) *Römische Kunst*, Weimar.

Krautheimer, R. (1965) *Early Christian and Byzantine Architecture*, Harmondsworth, Mx: Penguin.

La Baume, P. (n.d.) *The Romans on the Rhine*, 2nd edn, Bonn.

La Rocca, De Vos, M. and De Vos A. (1976) *Guida archeologica di Pompeii*, Milan: Mondadori.

Laurence, R. (1994) *Roman Pompeii: Space and Society*, London: Routledge.

Lawrence, A. W. (1929) *Classical Sculpture*, London: Cape.

Le Corbusier (1928) *Towards an Architecture*, London.

Leacroft, H. and Leacroft, R. (1969) *The Buildings of Ancient Rome*, Leicester: Brockhampton Press; New York: William R. Scott.

Ling, R. (1992) *Roman Painting*, Cambridge/London: Cambridge University Press.

L'Orange, H. P. (1965) *Art Forms and Civic Life in the Late Roman Empire*, Princeton, NJ: Princeton University Press.

L'Orange, H. P. and Nordhagen, P. J. (1966) *Mosaics*, London: Methuen.

Macdonald, W. L. (1986 [1965]) *The Architecture of the Roman Empire*, 2 vols, New Haven, CT: Yale University Press.

MacKendrick, P. (1962) *The Greek Stones Speak*, London: Methuen; 2nd edn 1981, New York/London: Norton.

MacKendrick, P. (1969) *The Iberian Stones Speak*, New York: Funk & Wagnall.

MacKendrick, P. (1975) *The Dacian Stones Speak*, Chapel Hill, NC: University of North Carolina Press.

Maclendon, C. M. (ed.) (1986) *Rome and the Provinces: Studies in the Transformation of Art and Architecture in the Mediterranean World* (symposium), New Haven, CT: Yale University Press.

McKay, A. G. (1975) *Houses, Villas and Palaces in the Roman World*, London: Thames & Hudson.

McNally, S. (1994) *American Journal of Archaeology* 98.

Macready, S. and Thompson, F. M. (eds) (1987) *Roman Architecture in the Greek World*, London: Society of Antiquaries.

Maiuri, A. (1953) *Roman Painting*, Geneva: Skira.

Mansuelli, G. A. (1966) *Etruria and Early Rome*, trans. C. E. Ellis, London: Methuen.

Mansuelli, G. A., Laurenzi, C. and Lagona, S. (1979) *Arte romana: pittura, arti minori*, Rome.

Mariani, L. and de Tomasi, G. (eds) (1993) *Pompei: la città scomparsa*, Naples.

Mattingly, H. (1928) *Roman Coins*, London: Methuen; reprinted 1960, 1962.

Mattingly, H. and Sydenham, E. A. (1930) *Roman Imperial Coinage*, London: Spink.

Medri, M. (1992) *Terra sigillata tardo-italica decorata*, Rome: Erma di Bretschneider.

Meiggs, R. (1974 [1960]) *Roman Ostia*, Oxford/London: Oxford University Press.

Milburn, R. (1988) *Early Christian Art and Architecture*, Berkeley/Los Angeles, CA: University of California Press.

Moorman, E. M. (ed.) (1992) *Functional and Spatial Analysis of Wall Painting*, Amsterdam.

Nielsen, I. (1993) *Thermae et Balnea; The Architecture and Cultural History of Roman Public Baths*, Aarhus: Aarhus University Press.

Niemeyer, H. G. (1968) *Studien zur statuarischen Darstellung der Römischen Kaiser*, ed. H. Kaehler, Vol. VII of Monumenta Artis Romanae, Berlin.

O'Connor, C. (1994) *Roman Bridges*, Cambridge/London: Cambridge University Press.

Ogden, J. (1992) *Ancient Jewellery*, London: British Museum.

Painter, K. S. (1977) *The Mildenhall Treasure*, London: British Museum.

Parlasca, K. (1966) *Mumienporträts und verwandte Denkmäler*, Wiesbaden: Steiner; Italian edn, 1977.

Pereira, M. (1968) *Istanbul*, London: Bles.

Peters, W. J. J. *Landscape in Romano-Campanian Mural Painting*, Assen: Van Gorcum.

Pevsner, N. (ed.) (1943) *Outline of European Architecture*, Harmondsworth, Mx: Penguin.

Pietrangeli, C. (1958) *Scavi e scoperte di antichita sotto il pontificato i Pio IV*, 2nd edn, Rome.

Pirzio Biroli Stefanelli, L. (ed.) (1990) *L'argento dei romani*, Rome: L'Erma.

Pirzio Biroli Stefanelli, L. (ed.) (1991) *L'oro dei Romani*, Rome.

Pobe, M. (1961) *The Art of Roman Gaul*, London: Readers' Union; reprinted 1962.

Pollitt, J. J. (1966) *The Art of Rome, c. 753 BC–AD 337: Sources and Documents*, Englewood Cliffs, NJ: Prentice-Hall; Cambridge/London: Cambridge University Press, 1983.

Pompeii. AD 79 (exhibition), London: Royal Academy of Arts, 1976–7.

Potter, T. W. and Johns, C. (1992) *Roman Britain*, London: British Museum Press.

Poulsen, V. (1962) *Les portraits romains*, Copenhagen: Ny Carlsberg Glyptothek Museum.

Quennell, P. (1971) *The Colosseum*, New York: Newsweek.

Radulescu, A. (n.d.) *Das Siegesdenkmal von Adamklissi*, Bucharest.

Ragghianti, G. (1963) *Pittori di Pompei*, Milan.

Ramage, N. H. and Ramage, A. (1991) *Roman Art*, Cambridge/London: Cambridge University Press.

Raven, S. (1993) *Rome in Africa*, 3rd edn, London: Routledge.

Reutersward, P. (1960) *Studien zur Polychromie der Plastik*, Stockholm: Almqvist & Wiksell.

Richmond, I. A. (1963) 'Palmyra under the aegis of the Romans', *Journal of Roman Studies* LIII.

Richmond, I. A. (1965) *Swan's Hellenic Cruises: Handbook for 1965*, London: Swan.

Richter, G. M. A. (1971) *Engraved Gems of the Romans*, London: Phaidon.

Richter, G. M. A. (1949) *Roman Portraits*, New York: Metropolitan Museum of Art.

Ridgway, B. S. (1989) *Roman Copies of Greek Sculpture: The Problem of the Originals*, Ann Arbor, MI: University of Michigan Press.

Rivet, A. L. F. (1988) *Gallia Narbonensis*, London: Batsford.

Rizzo, G. E. (1929) *La pittura ellenistico-romana*, Milan: Treves.

Robert, C. (ed.) (1897–1970) *Die antiken Sarkophag-Reliefs*, Rome.

Robertson, D. S. (1969) *Greek and Roman Architecture*, 2nd edn, Cambridge/London: Cambridge University Press.

Robinson, D. M. (1946) *Baalbek, Palmyra*, New York: Augustin.

Rodenwaldt, G. (1927) *Der Kunst der Antike*, Berlin: Propyläen Verlag.

Roman Portrait Busts, London: Arts Council, 1953.

Rosenthal, R. (1973) *Jewellery in Ancient Times*, London: Cassell.

Rossi, L. (1971) *Trajan's Column and the Dacian Wars*, London: Thames & Hudson; Ithaca, NY: Cornell University Press.

Rostovtzeff, M. (1960) *Rome*, New York/Oxford: Oxford University Press.

Rozenberg, S. (1994) *Enchanted Landscapes: Wall Paintings from the Roman Era*, London: Thames & Hudson.

Schefold, K. (1961) *Pompeji: Zeugnisse griechischer Malerei*, Munich: Piper.

Schefold, K. (1964) *Römische Kunst als religiöses Phänomen*, Reinbeck bei Hamburg: Rowohlt Taschenbuch Verlag.

Schefold, K. (1972) *La peinture pompéienne*, Brussels: Latomus.

Schlumberger, D. (1964) *L'orient hellenisé: l'art grec et ses héritiers dans l'Asie non-méditerranéenne*, Paris: Albin Michel.

Schoppa, H. (1957) *Die Kunst der Römerzeit in Gallien, Germanien und Britannien*, Munich/ Berlin: Deutscher Kunstverlag.

Sergejenko, M. J. (1955) *Pompeji*, 3rd edn, Leipzig: Koehler & Amelung.

Shore, A. F. (1962) *Portrait Painting from Roman Egypt*, London: British Museum.

Somerville, M. (1889) *Engraved Gems*, Philadelphia, PA.

Squarciapino, M. F. (1943) *La scuola di Afrodisias*, Rome: Governatorato di Roma.

Stenico, A. (1963) *Die Malerei in Alterthum*, Vol. II, Gütersloh: Bertelsman.

Stoneman, R. (1992) *Palmyra and its Empire*, Ann Arbor, MI: University of Michigan Press.

Strong, D. E. (1961) *Roman Imperial Sculpture*, London: Tiranti.

Strong, D. E. (1966) *Greek and Roman Gold and Silver Plate*, London: Methuen.

Strong, D. E. (1976) *Roman Art*, Harmondsworth Mx: Penguin

Strong, D. E. and Brown, D. (1976) *Roman Crafts*, London: Duckworth.

Strong, E. S. (1907–11) *Roman Sculpture from Augustus to Constantine*, London; Italian edn, Florence, 1923–6.

Strong, E. S. (1929) *Art in Ancient Rome*, London: Heinemann.

Summerson, J. (1963) *The Classical Language of Architecture*, London: BBC.

Sutherland, C. H. V. (1955) *Art in Coinage*, London: Batsford.

Swinder, M. H. (1929) *Ancient Painting*, New Haven, CT: Yale University Press.

Sydow, W. von (1969) *Zur Kunstgeschichte der Spätantiken Porträts in 4 Jh.n. Chr.*, Bonn: Rudolf Habelt Verlag.

Sztuka Palmyry (conference), Warsaw: Museum Narodowe in Warszawie, 1986.

Thomas, R. (1993) *Römische Wandmalerei in Köln*, Mainz: Von Zabern.

Thompson, D. L. (1976) *The Artists of the Mummy Portraits*, Malibu, CA: J. Paul Getty Museum.

Tomlinson, R. A. (1994) *Greek and Roman Architecture*, London: British Museum.

Torelli, M. (1982) *Typology and Structure of Roman Historical Reliefs*, Ann Arbor, MI: University of Michigan Pres.

Toynbee, J. M. C. (1951) *Some Notes on Artists in the Roman World*, Brussels.

Toynbee, J. M. C. (1964) *Art in Roman Britain*, Oxford: Clarendon Press.

Toynbee, J. M. C. (1965) *The Art of the Romans*, London: Thames & Hudson.

Toynbee, J. M. C. (1971) *Death and Burial in the Roman World*, Ithaca, NY: Cornell University Press.

Toynbee, J. M. C. (1978) *Roman Historical Portraits*, London: Thames & Hudson.

Toynbee, J. M. C. (1986 [1944]) *Roman Medallions*, amended reprint (with bibliographical introduction and emendation to plates by W. E. Metcalf), New York: American Numismatic Society.

Vermeule, C. (1968) *Roman Imperial Art in Greece and Asia Minor*, Cambridge, MA: Belknap Press.

Vermeule, C. (1977) *Greek Sculpture and Roman Taste* (Jerome Lecture), Ann Arbor, MI: University of Michigan Press.

Vermeule, C. (1979) *Roman Art: Early Republic to Late Empire*, Cambridge, MA: Harvard University Press.

Vermeule, C. (1986) *Greek Imperial Art: Numismatic Art of the Greek Imperial World*, Cambridge, MA: Harvard University Press.

Vickers, M. and Gill, D. W. (1994) *Artful Crafts: Ancient Greek Silverware and Pottery*, Oxford: Clarendon Press.

Wacher, J. (ed.) (1987) *The Roman World*, 2 vols, London: Routledge & Kegan Paul.

Walker, S. (1991) *Roman Art*, London: British Museum.

Walker, S. and Cameron, A. (eds) (1989) *The Greek Renaissance in the Roman Empire*, London: Bulletin of the Institute of Classical Studies, Suppl. 55.

Wallace-Hadrill, A. (1994) *Houses and Society in Pompeii and Herculaneum*, Princeton, NJ: Princeton University Press.

Walters, H. B. (1911) *The Art of the Romans*, London: Methuen; reprinted 1928.

Ward-Perkins, J. B. (1992) *Roman Imperial Architecture*, New Haven, CT: Yale University Press; reprint comprising Parts 2, 3, and 4 of Boethius' *Etruscan and Roman Architecture*, ed. J. B. Ward-Perkins.

Warmington, B. H. (1960) *Carthage*, London: Robert Hale.

Wegner, M. *et al.* (1939) *Das römische Herrscherbild*, Berlin: Mann.

Wells, C. M. (1984) *The Roman Empire*, 2nd edn, Stanford, CA: Stanford University Press.

West, R. (1941 [1933]) *Römische Porträtplastik*, 2 vols, Munich: Bruckmann.

Wheeler, R. E. M. (1964) *Roman Art and Architecture*, London: Thames & Hudson.

Wilkes, J. J. (1993 [1986]) *Diocletian's Palace, Split: Residence of a Roman Emperor*.

Wilkinson, L. P. (1981) *The Roman Experience*, Lanham, MD: University Press of America.

Williams, D. and Ogden, O. (1994) *Greek Gold: Jewellery of the Classical World*, London: British Museum.

Wilson, E. (1994) *8000 Years of Ornament*, London: British Museum.

Wilson, R. J. A. (1983) *Piazza Armerina*, Austin, TX: University of Texas Press.

Woodford, S. (1982) *The Art of Greece and Rome*, Cambridge/London: Cambridge University Press.

Woodford, S. (1992 [1982]) *The Cambridge Introduction to Art: Greece and Rome*, Cambridge/London: Cambridge University Press.

Yadin, Y. (1966) *Masada*, New York: Random House.

Yegül, F. (1992) *Baths and Bathing in Classical Antiquity*, Boston, MA: Massachusetts Institute of Technology.

Zaloscer, H. (1961) *Porträts aus dem Wustensand*, Vienna: Schroll.

Zanker, P. (1974) *Klassizistische Studien: Studien zur Veränderung das Kunstgeschmacks in der römischen Kaiserzeit*, Mainz.

Zanker, P. (1983) *Provinzielle Kaiserporträts: Zur Rezeption der Selbstdarstellung des Princeps* (Bayerische Akademie der Wissenschaften, Philosophische-historische Classe), Munich.

Zanker, P. (1987) *Pompeji: Stadtbilder als Spiegel von Gesellschaft und Herrschaftsform* (Trierer Winckelmannsprogramm), Mainz.

Zanker, P. (1990 [1988]) *The Power of Images in the Age of Augustus*, Ann Arbor, MI: University of Michigan Press.

Zevi, F. (ed.) (1991–2) *Pompei*, Vols I and II, Naples.

Zozoff, P. (1983) *Die antiken Gemmen* (Handbuch der Archäologie), Munich.

INDEX